A Manual for all Sea Kayakers

SEA KAYAK
SAFETY AND RESCUE

GORDON BROWN

Pesda Press LTD

www.pesdapress.com

Front cover: *Rescue in a cave, West Skye.*

Back cover: *Two's company, three would be ridiculous.*

First published in Great Britain 2019 by Pesda Press
Tan y Coed Canol
Ceunant
Caernarfon
Gwynedd
LL55 4RN

ISBN: 9781906095635

Printed and bound in Poland, www.hussarbooks.pl

DEDICATION

This book is dedicated to the memory of Duncan R Winning OBE, always a true and honest friend who gave his time and knowledge freely.

About the author

Gordon has recently moved from the Isle of Skye in Scotland to Vancouver Island in Canada. He has a lifetime's experience of kayaking in all its forms and well over thirty years of coaching sea kayaking. In 1992 he completed both sea kayak and white water kayak BCU Level 5 coach qualifications, and was involved in the development, training and assessment of these awards until they were discontinued when the award scheme was reorganised. In 2016 he completed a Masters Degree in Performance Coaching and has produced a set of three instructional DVDs in the *Sea Kayak with Gordon Brown* series, the world's first sea kayak rescue video, *Over ... and Out*, as well as writing the book *Sea Kayak,* also by Pesda Press.

Gordon believes that everyone has the potential to achieve more, and that a creative and supportive environment can lay the foundations for the greatest advances in personal development. He values the importance of taking time to reflect and learn from the experience. His most rewarding experiences are when helping someone else achieve their potential.

He likes acoustic folk music, close friends and good food although not necessarily in that order.

Gordon has previously said that he has the best job in the world. He still believes that to be true and looks forward to his time on the water with all students.

Photo: Angus Mackie

THANKS AND ACKNOWLEDGEMENTS

Thanks are due to very many people who have helped shape this book – any omissions are my fault alone and I extend my sincerest apologies to you if you feel missed out. To all of the students I have learned from over the years, a huge thank you. The photographers who were patient with my requests: Angus Mackie of Scotland 360, Kate Duffus, Mark Boyd, Michaela MacDonald, Roger Aguirre Smith and Rowland Woollven – many thanks, your work has made this book better. The many friends and paddlers who responded to my requests, as well as those of the photographers, thank you.

To all the team at Pesda Press for their encouragement, cajoling, timely reminders and artistry; you bring a special magic to everything you touch, thank you.

Morgan at North Water in Vancouver for being generous with time and products for testing.

Sean at the McMurdo Group for supplying a PLB for evaluation and teaching purposes.

The companies who sponsor my endeavours:

Kokatat for supplying clothing that exceeds expectations;

Valley Sea Kayaks for supplying kayaks that work for me;

Werner Paddles for supplying paddles to power my fun.

For my children, Kirsty, Eilidh and Iain, who make it all worthwhile.

Finally, a huge thank you to Morag, my long-suffering wife, who guides me, reads and comments on everything, and generally forces me to focus.

All images by Gordon Brown unless individually credited.

Gordon using VHF. Photo: Rowland Woollven

Introduction

"MAYDAY, MAYDAY, MAYDAY, this is Sea Kayak Gordon, Sea Kayak Gordon, Sea Kayak Gordon.

MAYDAY, Sea Kayak Gordon.

My position is one mile due west of the Skye Bridge.

I have one unconscious person in the water and require immediate assistance.

We are a group of four kayakers.

Over."

"Mayday, Sea Kayak Gordon, Stornoway Coastguard, say again your position over ..."

It was a normal day out. There was nothing to indicate that this day would be any different from the others. We were two groups; one of six almost complete beginners and another of three who had some experience and certification. Both groups were led by experienced coaches and shared the same plan – paddling a mostly sheltered downwind run of about six miles with a stop for lunch at the most protected place on the way.

I led the more experienced group, which comprised Tom, Dick and Sally and we worked on how to turn the kayaks in the wind before setting off. There were several places in the first mile where the wind was strong enough to make turning awkward and we exploited these opportunities. The group were controlling their kayaks well enough to journey the quarter-mile to an island, which was in a more exposed situation. From there, we returned to the coast to meet the other group for lunch. On the way, the group continued to develop the control of their kayaks with the wind from the side.

After lunch the groups separated again with the plan of meeting up at the car park in Kyleakin to share transport back to base. There were a couple of headlands where the wind was creating waves but these were no bigger than 20cm. So far, so good, but things were about to change.

In the bay before the second headland, one of the experienced group members, Dick, capsized and exited his kayak. He attempted a self rescue but failed and I helped him back into his kayak. When Dick's spraydeck was back on, I went to help Tom who was struggling to keep off the rocks. Once clear of the headland I looked behind me and saw that Dick was back in the water, out of his kayak. I gave the other two group members instructions to keep together and paddle into the sheltered area behind the rock, which was less than fifty metres away, and wait for me to return.

I went back to Dick, performed another rescue and escorted him towards the other two. Upon reaching the next small headland, I saw the upturned hull of one kayak and Sally attempting to pull Tom upright, using a type of rescue known as a 'Hand of God'. They were approximately two hundred metres from my position. I gave very specific instructions to Dick who was beside me. "Paddle carefully towards where I will be, while you support yourself, making sure that you stay upright." The last thing I needed was another capsize.

As I approached, Sally succeeded in pulling Tom all the way upright from his upside-down position, but due to Sally being off balance, having struggled for some time and not expecting to pull Tom upright, they fell inwards towards each other and both capsized. Sally stayed in her kayak and held on to Tom's upturned kayak while attempting to keep his head above the surface as much as possible. I paddled past the two discarded paddles and grabbed onto Tom's buoyancy aid pulling his head above the water and instructed Sally to exit her kayak.

By the blue-tinged colour of Tom's face, it was obvious that he was in poor shape. He didn't respond to his name being called and made no eye contact, but fortunately his coughing, gurgling, gasping breaths at least indicated that he was still breathing. With Sally in the water holding onto the front of my kayak, Dick coming towards us carefully and me holding onto the casualty, I took out my VHF radio and made a MAYDAY call to the coastguard. Between keeping Tom's head above the water, talking with the coastguard and guiding a nearby fishing boat towards our position, I was instructing Dick's rescue of Sally. When the rescue was complete, I told both Dick and Sally to go to shore, land and wait for me. By now we were only around 150 metres from shore. I released Tom's spraydeck and got him into the water ready to be lifted onto the fishing boat. Suddenly, a great skua or bonxie landed on the bow of my kayak. I have never had one of these birds land on my kayak before and I thought it was a bit ironic that this piratical scavenger should choose now to have a rest so close to the semi-conscious casualty. The bonxie flew off as the boat arrived.

Unfortunately, the fishing boat could not come alongside as it was too shallow. I manoeuvred Tom into his cockpit and pulled him upright by using a type of rescue known as a 'scoop' and with the casualty draped over my deck, reverse paddled into deeper water to where the fishing boat was waiting. Holding onto the fishing boat and Tom was awkward as the boat was rolling quite a bit. Its rubbing strake was hitting my shoulder every time it rolled towards me.

The lifeboat radioed their ETA, just one minute away, so I made the decision to remove myself from the fishing boat and await the lifeboat. At this moment, the other group came around the corner and assumed that I had been helping the fishing boat with some problem or other. When they saw the lifeboat approach, their coach instructed them to go ashore to where the others were.

With the casualty safely on the lifeboat, I connected a tow to Tom's kayak and made my way to shore to join the group.

Tom was transferred from the lifeboat to a waiting ambulance and taken to hospital for treatment, including a 24 hour stay on high-flow oxygen.

During a telephone debrief with the coastguard later, I was informed that it took 16 minutes from the time of my MAYDAY call until the lifeboat arrived on the scene, and a further 25 minutes until the casualty was in hospital.

Tom was fortunate. I'd trained for this eventuality for many years. The coastguard was able to pick up my MAYDAY call. There was a fishing boat close by. The lifeboat was about two miles from our location. It could have been so different. Frankly, Tom could have died.

Whatever made you stop, pick up and buy this book is not important. What is important is the fact that you have picked it up and have started to read through it. The lessons contained within the stories at the start of each chapter are designed to give an introduction to the techniques about to be discussed. There are mistakes described within these stories, some are real-life incidents reported as they happened, while others are second hand and perhaps embellished over the years of telling. All are designed to be thought provoking and help you, the reader, develop appreciation of some of the things that can go wrong when paddling on the sea. By paying attention to these stories, you will be developing awareness of the type of incident you may have to deal with when out by yourself or with your friends.

Photo: Rowland Woollven

The oceans of the earth are a serious and unforgiving environment and one where conditions can change very rapidly, from benign to extreme within minutes. Sea kayaking is not without risk, and incidents can, and do, occur. Dealing with these incidents is a stressful physical activity that takes place in a dynamic environment in real time. Additionally, the mental strain during the incident is huge, and attention can often be focused only on the casualty and not on the bigger picture.

When considering sea kayak safety and rescue it would be simplistic to think only of the hard skills and mechanics of rescuing yourself or someone else. That is only the tip of the iceberg. The underlying safety processes are often forgotten, meaning that many people may make the same, or similar, mistakes time and time again. A seemingly simple incident can quickly escalate into an emergency situation, perhaps putting life at risk, and requiring the assistance of outside agencies, such as in the true story you've just read.

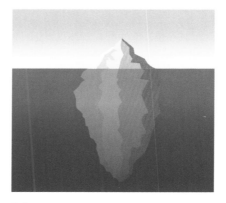

Iceberg.

By developing an understanding of the complexity of incidents, as well as how to limit their potential escalation by using decision-making processes, you will be able to avoid many incidents or, at the very least, nip them in the bud. In the following chapters we will look at these processes and how to put them in place. Anxiety, fear, decision making and observation are all areas which have been written about by experts. At the end of the book there is a bibliography of accessible writing and papers from journals which I have enjoyed reading.

All of the techniques in this book are intended to be used, tried, tested and adapted by anyone reading it. You cannot cross an ocean by standing on a beach looking at the water. Likewise, it is not possible to learn purely from a book something that is practical in application; however it does go a long way to help. To turn these techniques into skills requires deliberate practice. To apply them skilfully requires using them in the context of the conditions paddled.

Photo: Kate Duffus

Throughout the book, I have chosen to use 'casualty' to describe the person being rescued. Although not strictly the correct usage in the English language, it is the term used by the lifeboat teams and I prefer it to 'victim', which has undertones of a targeted incident by a perpetrator. 'Rescuer' is used to indicate the person carrying out the technique. In most of the stories, the names of the participants have been changed.

By thinking ahead and realising that safety is something we have the ability to influence, it is possible to avoid many fairly common incidents. A list of common and less common incidents is included at the end of the book. There is no one right answer for every situation. Instead, for each incident, there are usually several correct solutions, though sometimes just one will be completely obvious.

I hope the worst doesn't happen. If it does, I hope that after reading this book you will be better prepared to help yourself and those around you.

CONTENTS

Duncan Winning at the end of our trip.

Safety

It was all so easy. Duncan and I paddled for a month in Greenland and the only thing we had any issue with was pasta. I love the stuff and Duncan doesn't care too much about it. We found this out on the first night and just adapted our meals to suit. Fortunately, I had taken enough variety that it was not a problem.

Everything else worked out well. The kayaks were waiting for us in Ummannaq; Duncan's was damaged but we had packed resin and cloth in case of this eventuality. We set off and when we arrived at the village of Igdlorssuit on Ubekendt Island we were met by the local schoolchildren. The kids ran off to get the only person in the village who spoke any English, and Duncan was surprised when the woman who arrived was Elizabeth Fleischer, the person he had been communicating with for several months when we were planning our trip. She had worked in the tourist office in Illulissat while she was training to be a teacher and was now at her school. Having our own interpreter made communications so much easier. We were treated like royalty during our extended stay in the village and I was pretty sad when it came time to leave and continue our journey.

We had planned every part of our journey as best as we could from home, and now that we were in a country with cultural and language differences, everything just worked out fine. I hate to think what would have happened if we had just arrived and set off. By studying the charts extensively, I had a picture in my head of the relationship of all the islands as well as where the villages and hunters' camps would be. Anticipating that the kayaks could be damaged in transit to Uummannaq, we sent enough repair materials (resin, cloth, skeg wire, screws, shock cord, deck line etc.) in the kayaks to allow us to join a broken kayak and also carry out any other repairs that could be required. We had made sure our food would be suitable to last the month and give us enough energy to stay warm. By communicating with the closest tourist office to our destination, we had someone who knew who we were, where we were going and what we were trying to do.

THINKING ABOUT SAFETY

Safety is a state of mind.

There are three main areas of importance when thinking about safety; these are Self / Group, Task and Environment.

Self / Group – Taking care of one's own mental and physical well-being is an important step towards developing good self-respect. When we respect ourselves, we tend to make better decisions. Knowing and understanding why we do something is as important as being able to do that something. Having a good positive attitude will go a long way to solving a problem, often before it even becomes a problem.

There is no doubt that paddling in a supportive, coherent group feels, and usually is, much safer but it can, and often does, lead to a false sense of security. Good communications and appropriate leadership are essential. The main risk in a group, if no one is keeping an eye out for everyone, is that there comes a time when there is some sort of breakdown within the group. This may not be a catastrophic failure, just some simple misunderstanding that can lead to a cascade effect and everything just gets worse. We can prevent this happening.

Task – The task is what we / the group sets out to do. It is important to think about safety when setting the task; is the task suited to the conditions? Are all the members of the group able to complete it? Choosing a complex task in difficult conditions may be appropriate if it has been previously attempted in more benign conditions.

Setting a task beyond our ability would place a vast amount of stress, both mental and physical, on the members of the group. The risk would be that a fairly straightforward task in easy conditions would become almost impossible. The more prepared we are, the better we will be able to cope with situations that arise.

Environment – The sea is a fantastic playground, and one which is constantly changing. Imagine playing chess in the normal fashion; there is you, your opponent and the board with the pieces on it. Now try to picture a four dimensional chessboard, which is constantly changing and where the pieces also change form and ability. The ocean, where we sea kayakers operate, is a real-life, ever-changing chessboard, without rules. It will challenge everyone who sets out to explore it and make a fool out of anyone who does not plan and think ahead.

Chessboard.

FORETHOUGHT AND PLANNING

By thinking ahead and planning your trip, taking into account the group, the weather forecast and the tides, you have gone a long way to preventing things going wrong in the first place.

For example, arriving at a headland at slack water rather than a few hours later at full flood, is easily predicted and planned for. Ensuring everyone has enough food, warm clothing and a head lamp could be the difference between spending a miserable time on the water after darkness has fallen and having an amazing experience.

OBSERVATION AND AWARENESS

By being observant and aware of the sea and its changing moods, and your fellow paddlers, you are able to deal with a minor problem before it develops into a major epic.

Things often start to go wrong much sooner than they become visible to us. By being observant and aware, you may see something coming early, then you can often prevent it happening, or at least be in a good position to deal with it.

For example, it is easy to miss the important cues that signal the onset of one capsize after another, or when navigating, it is very easy to mistake one specific place for another similar one close by. Sometimes these are not important, but at other times they are the start of things escalating into an incident.

PRACTISING SKILLS AND SCENARIOS

Having carefully evaluated, selected, maintained and practised using your equipment, as well as performed a variety of scenarios, you will be mentally and physically prepared to deal with most situations.

Time spent practising the skills discussed within this book will be time well spent as long as the practice closely resembles reality. The more realistic the recreated scenario is, the more likely you will be able to solve a similar issue if it should come up as a part of your everyday paddling. Many scenarios have similar components and often the same, or similar, approach will work in almost every case, but exceptions do happen. By putting a planned scenario under pressure of time or conditions, the simulation will be closer to a real-life, real-time incident. Practising when there is a safety net of other paddlers around, or in a sheltered location, is the safest method of changing the techniques into skills.

INDIVIDUAL ROLES AND EXPECTATIONS

It is always good to know what each person's role is within a group. Some people like to lead and are not happy unless they are doing so, others are content to take a back seat in everything, but there is a risk this will lead to them becoming ever more dependent on the other group members. Everyone should be encouraged to take responsibility for all aspects of the paddling, from the initial planning, to ensuring all the kit has been lifted from the landing site at the end of the journey.

It is possible to work at a much higher level when operating within a cohesive group, than as an individual who is out with other individuals. The collective organic knowledge of a group is substantially greater than that of an individual and, when combined, can bring about more satisfactory 'moves' being made on the chessboard.

COMMUNICATION

Everyone within a group has to be involved in communicating with everyone else. Communication can be problematic and every opportunity must be taken to ensure the message is received as intended.

- ◎ Don't be afraid to ask someone to repeat a message.
- ◎ Be prepared to check you have correctly understood by paraphrasing. For example, *"Let me see if I've got this right; what you want me to do is ..."*

LEARNING FROM EXPERIENCE

Incidents have happened in the past and will continue to do so in the future. This is not a good reason to stop doing the activity, as long as we can learn from the experiences of others and hopefully not make the same mistakes along the way.

Gathering information from other paddlers is a great way to develop awareness of the type of incidents that can happen on the sea, and should be encouraged as a means of preventing similar incidents in the future. Unfortunately, but understandably, people are often unwilling to openly share information about a specific incident, as they feel that it may result in criticism being directed at them and their actions.

Prevention is better than cure.

Group preparing to launch, North East Skye.

Sean Morley at Point Bonita.
Photo: Bob & Mieko Watkins

Assessing Risk

Risks (Attributed to William Arthur Ward 1921–1994)

To laugh is to risk appearing the fool.
To weep is to risk appearing sentimental.
To reach out for another is to risk involvement.
To expose feelings is to risk exposing your true self.
To place ideas and dreams before a crowd is to risk being called naive.
To love is to risk not being loved in return.
To live is to risk dying.
To hope is to risk despair.
To try is to risk failure.
But risk must be taken, because the greatest hazard in life is to risk nothing.
The person who risks nothing, does nothing, has nothing, is nothing and becomes nothing.
They may avoid suffering and sorrow, but they cannot learn, feel, change, grow, love, live.
Chained by their certitude, they are slaves; they have forfeited their freedom.
Only a person who risks is truly free.

As the writing above clearly states, taking risks is an inherent part of life. It is how we deal with what we find when we look at risk, that is of interest. Much has been written about risk assessment, risk management and risk benefit analysis but how does this actually translate to being on the sea in a sea kayak?

Risk is normally considered to be 'a situation that involves exposure to danger'. This is true, and if we were to sit down and write a list of all the things that could go wrong while we were sea kayaking, we would never go out! By exposing ourselves to risk, we can develop a better understanding of what is actual risk and what is not (real versus perceived risk). If we don't take risks then our development stops. Only by taking the time to work out what is real risk and what is perceived risk, can we truly understand risk and grow in our knowledge and judgement.

Perceived risk is almost completely governed by fear. The next chapter deals with this and how we can develop a healthy awareness of this primitive emotion.

Apsley Cherry-Garrard wrote in his book, *The Worst Journey in the World*, "*Generally the risks were taken, for, on the whole, it is better to be a little over-bold than a little over-cautious,*" and "*It is so easy to be afraid of being afraid*". The book is about Antarctic travel at the turn of the 1900s and specifically focuses on the winter journey made to Cape Crozier with Edward Wilson and Birdie Bowers.

ASSESSING RISK

A useful mnemonic when thinking about risk is:

R – Real

I – Imagined

S – Share your feelings / Show your vulnerabilities

K – Know your limits but push them

Everyone's perception of risk differs, and it is this that makes assessing what is risk and what is not, more difficult. Often the imagined risk is greater than the real risk and this creates a feeling of being out of control.

Thinking about rock hopping; some will state that it involves too much risk, while others who have enjoyed rock hopping see the benefit of exposing themselves to the same level of risk. Risk is subjective and cannot be measured in real terms. By focusing on the benefits of exposure to risk and managing it, rather than trying to eliminate risk completely, sea kayakers will be able to better determine what is real and what is perceived risk.

There is sometimes a misconception that formally assessing risk will lead to some form of control or prohibition. On the contrary, it will empower you to take the risks that will develop your paddling in a controlled and considered way.

In a group situation with a leader, it is much better that everyone becomes involved in the processes of identifying and managing risk. If the group members don't consider the risks involved, they won't learn how to deal with them and are not developing their own framework for assessing risk.

The following risk assessment models have been tried and tested and work well with groups in a sea kayaking context.

RISK TARGET

The risk target is a self-evaluation of each member of the group's perception of risk that allows the leader to have an overview of perceived risk.

On a sheet of paper, there are four areas: people, environment, weather and equipment. Each person involved in the plan has to indicate where on the red, yellow and green target, they are in relation to each area. When everyone scores themselves in the green sector, this means that all are content with the plan. A close eye still needs to be kept on developments during the outing, but otherwise it is a pretty safe place to be operating.

If some people are in the yellow zone, it means that they are not too happy with some part of the plan, this could be in any of the four areas and for any reason. Red is danger, and if anyone is in the red zone, there is quite possibly something wrong with the plan and it needs to be changed.

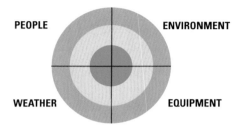

Illustration of the target.

People

The variables with people are many. It could be that someone has had a sleepless night, is starting to come down with some nasty bug, had too much to drink the previous night, has dropped their kayak, or anything else which may affect their mental state.

Environment

This area is about the physical environment in which the activity is about to take place and could be: surf, rock gardens, open crossing, exposure, lack of landing zones, or any other sea-related setting.

Weather or tide

This is the component that pervades all of the others and is the one where there are the most variables. Sometimes it is unpredictable; there could be local wind or tide anomalies, it could be a bigger than normal spring tide or a non-forecasted dramatic increase in wind speed.

Equipment

Of the four areas, this is the one where checks can easily be carried out before going afloat, to ensure there are few unexpected issues. Kayaks and paddles should be in reasonable condition with skegs or rudders operating correctly; all deck lines including toggle lines must be intact and not frayed; hatch covers securely fitted and tied on; towlines should conform to sensible norms; buoyancy aids must be worn and correctly adjusted.

This form of risk assessment can be done informally where appropriate. If launching from a sandy beach it is possible to draw the target in the sand and have people move around to show where their idea of risk is, regarding the activity. Care has to be taken though, as often individuals will follow others in their decision about where to place their mark, giving a false representation of where they perceive the risk to be. Honesty is required as any misrepresentation is likely to impact the safety of the whole group.

These four areas (people, environment, weather and equipment) were shown to be where things went wrong during sea kayaking activities according to a study of incidents (Brown, 2015).

RISK MATRIX

The risk matrix is a step up from the target, it is more specific, with leader-set questions that require answers. It also forms a checklist and memory jog for the group leader to ensure nothing is missed. Again, green is good, yellow signifies 'care needed', while red is an indication that there is perhaps a need for a change of plan.

RISK ASSESSMENT MATRIX	YES	DON'T KNOW	NO
Are all permissions (consent, NOK, ...) in place?			
Are you working within your remit?			
Is everyone able to carry out the plan?			
Do you have ALL of your equipment with you?			
Is everyone correctly equipped?			
Have you a designated Shore Based Contact (and left a float plan)?			
Have you got a weather forecast?			
Have you worked out Tides & Currents?			
Have you considered all other environmental variations?			
Is it safe to start the activity?			
SAFE TO GO AHEAD WITH PLAN			
CONSIDER, THINK, ACT			
STOP			

Risk matrix 1.

RISK AWARENESS FOR ALL

The risk target and matrix above are primarily for the leader. This final matrix is for everyone involved, not just the leader. If everyone is happy with all that is about to take place, then it's 'all systems go', if not there needs to be further discussion. This can seem overly formal, but having everyone sign to say they are happy, or unhappy, about the proposed plan should mean that they are better informed as to the real and perceived risks and will serve to make them better paddlers.

GROUP RISK ASSESSMENT		Tick the box next to your signature to show your opinion about the planned activity.		
Date:	Location:			
Leader:				
Planned Activity:				
Name	Signature	SAFE	NOT SURE	NOT SAFE

Risk matrix 2.

HSE MODEL

The Health and Safety Executive's model for risk assessment is used widely in industry. It has five steps: hazard identification, identifying those at risk, risk evaluation and control, recording of actions, and review of assessment. Unfortunately it is not adaptable enough for the dynamic environment of sea kayaking.

RISK AND THE SOLO PADDLER

Most paddlers who choose to go out by themselves are actually more aware of the risks involved than those who only venture out within the apparent safety of a group. They have rapidly developed a huge bank of knowledge over the time they have been paddling, and often will paddle at a much lower level when solo paddling than if they were out with a group. This is not always the case though, and many top-level paddlers push themselves well beyond what most people would consider safe, or sane.

A checklist, simplified into a series of bullet points is a good way to start the process of solo paddling.

- How am I feeling?
- Is this journey / activity within my skill set?
- Is the weather suitable?
- Are the tides favourable?
- Have I been here before?
- Have others been before me?
- Are there any hidden dangers?
- Have I let anyone know my plan?
- Do I have **everything** I need for safety?

There are others, though, who go out with almost zero knowledge or skills and somehow manage to 'get away with it'. To quote William (not Bill) Nealy, in his book *Kayak*, *"It is better to be lucky than good"*.

Nealy is of course being ironic. Chancers will eventually run out of luck. Consistent good luck is called ability.

Paddling solo can bring its own risks and rewards.

Fear.
Photo: Michaela MacDonald

Fear and Anxiety

I'm waiting for a friend to arrive. He emailed a couple of days ago to see if I would like to paddle a river with a group of 'over fifties', the only concession was that, "Egos get left in the cars".

I agreed as it meant getting out and meeting some of the locals. *But* ... I'm feeling anxious, perhaps verging on nervous and ask myself why? I've paddled a similar class of water many times over the last forty-odd years. I've paddled with people I don't know. I've coached and led on much more difficult water. I've not paddled white water for almost two years. Aha, that's it! I'm scared – scared of what others think, how others view me, scared that I'll not perform the way I want to, scared that I'll mess up and cause the others to have to work and help me. Yet, this is all just a part of the normal preparations to go onto the water. Fear and anxiety go hand in hand and often it is our fear of what we don't know that we fear.

I'm going out now and will reflect on this when I come back after our paddle ...

At the put-in my feelings of anxiety increased as one member of the group took charge and told us how we were going to paddle and the signals that we would use.

While on the water, I thought about how I had felt while waiting and about the 'flight, fight or freeze' response to danger or fear. I was definitely in the flight mode, my body was getting ready to run and get out of the situation it was in. I know that this is my default setting, and also that as soon as I am in the situation I have feared, that response disappears and I am able to enjoy being in the moment. I enjoyed the river, the company of the others and the good-natured banter that went along with it.

GOOD OR BAD FEAR

Good fear, fear that you can control, is stimulating and can be thought of as 'arousal'. Bad fear is uncontrolled, or uncontrollable, fear that can lead to panic or paralysis. It is possible to learn to control our fears and use the resulting aroused state to our advantage.

WHAT IS FEAR?

Fear is a deep-seated response or emotion to any situation that is likely to cause pain, is threatening or is dangerous. It can increase performance as well as be completely debilitating, depending on the cause of the fear and the possible outcomes. Our brains are not very good at sifting the good from the bad when it comes to fear, and often our minds race ahead to reach a conclusion that doesn't even exist.

FEAR OF THE UNKNOWN

Fear of the unknown, or the anticipated, is quite possibly the most debilitating kind of fear. Because we do not know what is likely to happen, the unknown element is always lurking in the background, just waiting for the right moment to surface. This is almost completely irrational. If the 'thing' is outside of our control and we can do nothing about it, we shouldn't even consider fearing it.

FEAR OF THE KNOWN

This is the one that we are able to deal with and is the rational fear that comes about through experience of what is right and what is not. When we are anxious, many things happen to our performance. Our sight / vision becomes narrower and more focused on a 'spot'. Our heart rate increases, as does our breathing rate. Our subconscious brain is working out whether to:

◎ freeze and hope that whatever it is that is making us feel this way will just go away,

◎ stand and fight so that we can get back to what we were doing before we felt this way, or

◎ turn and run away.

No matter which option is facing us, the aim is to change the situation we find ourselves in. If the situation you are in has been developing for a considerable time, then extracting yourself from it could take some time too.

ANXIETY

Almost any time there is an uncertain outcome, there will be some form of anxiety. Anxiety is normal; everyone feels anxious sometime. Whether standing in front of people giving a presentation, about to paddle in strong winds or standing on the shore thinking about how you feel.

Anxiety is not dangerous to us; it is a normal, uncomfortable emotion designed to keep us safe from harm and protect us from danger. It is temporary – for most people it does not usually last beyond a few minutes; and anonymous – others looking at you seldom know it is happening.

Anxiety does affect how we think – we typically have a fear of something really bad happening, and our body gives us signs in the form of thoughts, behaviours and physical symptoms. How we interpret these will determine how we respond.

If we think of anxiety as an early warning system, or precursor to fear, we can start to use the arousal developed to enhance our performance, but if there is no real danger, it can be exhausting.

FLIGHT, FIGHT OR FREEZE RESPONSE

The flight, fight or freeze response is a natural alarm system contained in our brain; it was hard-wired into our ancestors long before they were capable of rational thought. It can occur when there is either real or perceived danger. Often, instead of learning to deal with it, people stop doing the things that make them feel anxious and this can sometimes increase the response. We don't want to stop anxiety as it protects us from real danger, but we do need to calibrate it in order for us to perform well.

When we are anxious our body produces adrenaline, and this causes sensations which are known as the 'alarm reaction'.

PHYSICAL SYMPTOMS

Increase in pulse and breathing rate – to ensure that major muscles are ready to allow you to run, or stay and fight, as more blood and oxygen are circulated.

Sweating – it cools the body.

Nausea and upset stomach – anxiety can cause diarrhoea, nausea and feelings of having an upset stomach. This is due to the body shutting down various processes, which are superfluous in times of survival. Digestion is not needed when in danger.

Lightheaded or dizzy feeling – as most of the oxygen in the system is being directed to the arms and legs to allow us to fight or take flight, there is a slight decrease in blood flow and oxygen to the brain.

Tightness in chest – as you prepare for action, your muscles start to tense up.

Tingling and numbness – hyperventilation (very quick breathing) forces too much oxygen into our system and this can cause numbness and tingling sensations. Extremities do not need as much blood or oxygen so this is redirected to the bigger muscles. Our hair also stands on end and increases our sensitivity to movement and touch.

Brighter vision – our pupils dilate when we respond to danger. This is to let more light in and allows us to see more clearly. Sometimes what we are looking at can seem less real than normal, or it can appear slightly fuzzy.

Heavy arms and legs – as more blood is being pumped to our fight or flight muscles, these can feel heavy and unresponsive. There will also be increased muscle tension in the arms and legs.

BEHAVIOURS

Behaviour is under our control but when we become anxious there can be changes that are noticeable to others.

◎ We could feel uncomfortable, and this might display as fidgeting or nervousness.

◎ We may want to move out of the situation we are in as quickly as possible.

◎ We may alter our behaviour so as to try not to get into the situation in the first place.

◎ A belief that we are in danger could lead to us making poor decisions resulting in aggressiveness or other abnormal behaviour.

THOUGHTS

The belief that we are in danger always manages to surface, even if we are not in any actual danger. Other kinds of thoughts might include:

"Bad things are going to happen," almost to the point of superstition.

"What if I forget something important?"

PERFORMANCE AND FEAR

An optimal level of arousal is required to allow peak performance. When this threshold is exceeded, a dramatic, even catastrophic decrease in performance results. This peak performance threshold is completely individual and can be changed with continual practice and exposure to the arousal or anxiety components that are causing the threshold to manifest itself in the first place.

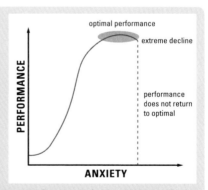

Catastrophe Curve, modified from Yerkes and Dodson.

As can be seen in the diagram above, performance increases as anxiety increases, until a point is reached where there is a window of optimal performance. If the anxiety, or arousal, increases further, there is an extreme decline in performance. No matter how much the performer reduces the arousal, the previous levels of performance cannot be achieved.

IMPROVING RESISTANCE TO ANXIETY, AND IMPROVING PERFORMANCE AS A RESULT

There are many thoughts that run through our heads as we become anxious. It is important to be able to recognise when this is happening, and develop a mechanism that allows competent performance even in an anxious state. By developing an understanding of how you respond to anxiety, you will be better prepared to deal with whatever happens. As an example, almost all of my reaction is in my stomach: the butterflies, the empty feeling that is like something has been taken from you, the not-quite-but-almost sick feeling.

As soon as I feel this starting, I ask myself three questions:

1. How bad is it really?

2. Have I done this before?

3. What is the worst that could happen?

If the worst thing that could happen is that I wet exit and perhaps take a bit of a beating, I know that there is little to fear. If I feel that I could get seriously injured, I will reconsider the activity, alter my plan, and revisit the three questions above until I am sure that I have made the correct decision.

By deliberately exposing yourself to controlled doses of risk, you start to learn how to deal with anxiety. This will increase your resistance to becoming anxious and improve your performance as a direct result. The signs of being anxious will still be present as your 'early warning system', but when recognised, they can be harnessed into positive, rather than negative, behaviour.

Boreray.

Paddling in a Group

I was leading a group of six clients, who were all friends, in the Loch Bracadale area on Skye. The sun was shining and the wind was from the north-east, light but forecast to increase slightly. We had met that morning and within the group there was a variety of sea kayaking experience, from someone who had paddled most weeks for the last ten years to one who had only been in a sea kayak once.

We stopped for lunch at the only landing place on the south side of the island of Wiay and decided that we would paddle to MacLeod's Maidens, a group of spectacular sea stacks two miles to the west. As we got afloat, we grouped together and started making our way along the cliff to where the gentle breeze would be on our right side.

Upon reaching the open water, it was obvious to me that the wind had increased much more than the forecast had suggested and that our plan would have to change. Unfortunately the group did not know this and before I could communicate the change of plan to them, one capsized and wet exited his kayak. I shouted to the others to turn their kayaks into the wind and hold position while I sorted out the rescue. The waves were about 75cm high.

One of the group had put his skeg down so his kayak was turning downwind constantly, which meant that he was heading offshore. Another was holding his course at about three knots. The others had turned into the wind. I had three different casualties to deal with, all at once; the one going downwind, the one going upwind and the one in the water. Fortunately, the other three were managing to keep their kayaks turned into the wind and close to the casualty in the water.

At this point, just in case the situation really got out of hand, I prepared for the option of making a mayday call. I took my VHF radio from my pocket, turned it on, selected channel 16 and made sure it was on high power.

I kept a lookout for the paddler turning downwind as I rescued the one in the water. I had less concern for the one heading into the wind, as I knew that his skill level would allow him to reach land in the increasingly sheltered conditions he was heading into, and also that if he did capsize, he would be blown towards us. With the rescue complete, I set up a rafted tow and took the group back into the lee of the island, before heading out for the downwind demon. When I got close enough to communicate that he should put his skeg up, he capsized. With this rescue completed and a contact tow underway, I then started thinking about the upwind flier who I could just see on the horizon, still going strong. As our intended campsite was on Wiay, and he had already passed it, I decided to get the main group to the campsite. Once they were ashore with instructions to set up their tents, get changed and get some hot drinks on the go, I was happy to head into the wind.

It took me close to 45 minutes of hard paddling to catch up with the sixth group member. He was very happy paddling into the wind but had not looked behind, until I asked where he thought he was in relation to the others. I'll never forget the look on his face when he saw the island in the distance. We paddled together, landed at our campsite and were given a mug of tea each. That night was great fun with a big fire and much laughter. I was drained though and headed off to bed early.

WHO IS IN CHARGE?

This is an interesting question and one that many peer group paddlers struggle with. There needs to be one person in control of the situation and this in itself can lead to frustrations within the group. As soon as there is any ego involved, especially with the leader, things start to unravel.

AGEISM AND SEXISM

In my experience, many people have problems with a leader who is younger, or that they perceive as less experienced than they are themselves.

Many men find that they struggle with a woman leading them, probably due to some atavistic idea that they themselves are stronger and more suited to leading.

Women often make good leaders because they are much more likely to listen to group members' thoughts and respect everyone's opinions, before making a considered decision on the outcome and the plans.

It makes some sense that the person in charge is also the one who is most experienced. However, if their chosen style of leadership is one that stifles experimentation, there will be less development and the other group members will not learn other leadership styles.

The larger the group, the more vital it is that it is made clear who is the leader, who takes responsibility in a given situation. The danger is that everybody assumes that somebody else has that covered. In very small groups this is less likely to be the case. If there are only two paddlers and one wet exits, it is fairly obvious who is in charge of the rescue.

In an informal group, people may be reluctant to put themselves forward for fear of being seen as 'pushy'. A way around this problem is to ask questions rather than give orders. For example:

"If we get into a rescue situation who is going to take control of the group?"

AWARENESS OF SELF

Knowing our own limits and abilities, especially the psychological ones, is an important aspect of paddling within a group. If we know how we react to being told what to do and when to do it, we may be able to minimise the stress caused when this happens.

It can sometimes be difficult to keep our enthusiasm in check within the confines of a group and often it is hard not to drift away to play in some feature or other. This applies whether we are a group member or a leader within the group.

AWARENESS OF OTHERS

Not knowing the other members of a group is one of the biggest challenges facing us, whether we are a full-time professional or a part-time club paddler. By having a deeper understanding and knowledge of our fellow sea kayakers, we can begin to make decisions based on their abilities and limits.

Often paddlers set their own limits and almost always at a lower level than their actual abilities. Sometimes though, there will be someone who believes that they are very much better than they really are, and this can cause much frustration within a group.

COMMUNICATION – VERBAL AND SIGNALS

A magnet on a friend's fridge reads: *"The biggest problem with communication is the illusion that it has taken place"*. In today's hi-tech world, we 'connect' with people mostly over some electronic device, but it is more important for us to be able to do it face-to-face. When sea kayaking, the ability to communicate is a fundamental skill, unless paddling alone, and even then it could be important when dealing with another person you come across. Communication takes many forms: verbal with other audible signals, or non-verbal with hand or paddle signals.

It is really important to avoid misunderstandings. At best this could be embarrassing and at worst, life threatening. One way of ensuring the message has been received as intended, is to ask the recipient to repeat the message back to you. Another is to ask a question about the message, the answers will reveal whether the message has been understood or not.

VISUAL SIGNALS

Verbal communication works well until the environment changes and the words disappear into the background noise. A set of internationally understood signals would be useful but they don't exist. I propose the following:

Are you okay? I'm okay.

Both the question and the response are the same.

One hand raised until the palm can be placed on top of the head.

No response means that the person is not all right and needs some assistance.

Are you okay? I'm okay.

Hold position

Everyone stops when safe and holds their position until the next signal.

Paddle held horizontally.

Hold your position until the next signal.

All come

Everyone come to my position.

Paddle held vertically.

Everyone come to my position.

Individual come

You, come to my position.

Point to an individual then hold the same hand vertically.

You, come to my position.

Go to

You, go over there.

Paddle, or hand, pointing towards the position the paddler has to go towards.

You, go over there (using the paddle to signal).   *You, go over there (using a hand to signal).*

Help needed

I need help.

Paddle or hand waved above head.

I need help (using the paddle to signal).   *I need help (using a hand to signal).*

*Using a
VHF radio.*

INTER-GROUP VHF

When using VHF radio for inter-group communications, the best option is for everyone to remain on channel 16, initialise contact on channel 16 then move to an agreed working channel. It helps if the working channel is agreed in advance. If everyone uses this standard protocol, everyone can hear what is going on.

The risk with the group choosing a channel other than 16 is highlighted in the following scenario. A member of the group becomes separated from the others in rough water. This person then capsizes and tries to call the other group members on his VHF radio but can't get through due to the noise. He then goes to channel 16 and broadcasts a mayday call which the others do not hear because they are listening in on a different channel. This mayday is picked up by outside rescue agencies and a search is initialised. The group members could be within communicating distance, but due to them not having their radios on channel 16 they do not know what is going on.

USING THE VHF RADIO WITH EXTERNAL AGENCIES

External agencies such as the coastguard are very professional, and will guide and encourage you to use correct radio protocol when using a VHF radio to communicate.

I encourage you to use your VHF to communicate with the coastguard whenever you venture onto the water. This will allow you to develop confidence and good radio procedure, before you need it in an emergency.

GROUP DYNAMICS

Many factors influence group dynamics. They can affect the coherent working of the group or even cause the group to disintegrate. Sometimes, it is down to one individual who feels that they are not able to do what they want, and at other times it is an overall feeling of unhappiness.

GROUP GOALS VERSUS INDIVIDUAL GOALS

As soon as the goals of an individual group member supersede the collective goals of the group, relationships will start to break down. Group goals are seldom written down but implicitly understood by the members.

EVERYONE LOOKS OUT FOR EVERYONE

Each group member is responsible for the wellbeing of all the other group members and must have their best interests at heart. Even when there is a designated leader, everyone should be aware of the mental and physical state of their paddling companions. For example, the leader could be so involved with leading that they fail to notice the subtle changes throughout the day which indicate that a group member is starting the decline towards hypothermia. This could easily be noticed by other group members. This can be improved by using the buddy system as described below in the section *Group control*. This way, in addition to generally keeping an eye on other group members, you are particularly responsible for your buddy, and your buddy for you.

MAINTAINING A GOOD RELATIONSHIP

Honesty, trust, respect and loyalty are the core principles of every relationship. Paddling in a group is a relationship and these principles have to be bi-directional.

Honesty is appreciated – if someone does not say that they are not feeling too good, how can this be accommodated within the plan? If you are not feeling good about something, you have to let others know.

Trust is gained – through being the very best you can be and always approachable, no matter what.

Respect is earned – by being true to yourself and your values.

Loyalty is returned – you can't expect someone to be loyal to you, if you are not loyal to them.

GROUP CONTROL

There are two ways of increasing group control and safety. One is formation paddling and the other is the much less formal, and far more flexible, buddy system. If a group needs to keep things really tight the two systems can be combined.

I remember when I was about twelve, paddling within a group. We were being led by two respected coaches and we had to paddle in formation all of the time, no matter what. This was explained to us as a method of providing safety. To the young me, this was incredibly boring and didn't allow me any chance of experimentation or real exploration, which is probably why I prefer to use a buddy system.

FORMATION PADDLING

Parallel lines

Form two parallel lines, the kayakers stay approximately half a kayak's length apart with one kayak's length in between. The two people at the rear are in a position to perform a rescue if someone capsizes. This technique relies on everyone being able to keep in formation. The best option is to place the less able group members at the front, this means that they dictate the pace of the whole group, with the more experienced ones, who are less likely to capsize, at the rear.

Two parallel lines formation.

Arrowhead

The person in the lead of the arrowhead formation should be either the least able group member, or a very able one who can turn around and be aware of where everyone is at all times. This leaves the leader free to move around the group and keep everyone together.

Arrowhead formation.

The remainder of the group follow on, just off to either side of the person in front but no more than five metres from anyone else. If someone capsizes, the person immediately behind and to one side is in a good position to effect a rescue.

Diamond

The diamond formation is similar to the arrowhead but is filled in with paddlers. I like this formation because whoever is in the centre of the group is able to rest slightly as they are sheltered by the people surrounding them. This method also allows the development of wash hanging (getting help from the wave created by another paddler) as a skill and allows a tired paddler to go faster than they could otherwise manage.

Diamond formation.

THE BUDDY SYSTEM

Using a buddy system is a good option for a leader, as it halves the number of people to be looked after. Instead of having to check for, say, six people, the leader now only has to look out for three pairs. Each buddy pair is responsible for itself within the bigger group. (With buddies being particularly responsible for each other, if someone is having problems it should not go unnoticed.) If something goes wrong, the buddy should alert the others before initiating a rescue or other help. This method of keeping the group together, though not quite as effective as formation paddling, does reduce the load on whoever is leading.

Three pairs of buddies.

HEALTH ISSUES

Health issues can be a sensitive matter and sometimes a group member does not disclose important information, maybe for fear that they will be banned from the activity.

It is everyone's responsibility to disclose relevant personal medical information, no matter how insignificant it may seem. Some conditions are obvious such as asthma, diabetes and epilepsy. Others may be less so, and although fairly insignificant in themselves, could be a sign that something else might be triggered. A good example is persistent indigestion, which could be a symptom of a heart-based problem. Another is a nagging sore back, as this could reduce the ability to carry out a rescue, or even limit that person's ability to be rescued.

EQUIPMENT

A problem that can occur in groups is that everyone assumes that someone else is carrying a particular item of equipment. In my view each person should carry a certain minimum amount of gear (see *Equipment* chapter). If certain items are considered group equipment, it has to be made very clear who is carrying them.

Everyone has to ensure that everyone else has all of the appropriate equipment to allow them to complete the proposed paddle in safety and comfort. The danger is that 'everyone' becomes 'no one'. In practice, someone has to take this responsibility. To help achieve this, a checklist could be compiled during the planning phase of the journey.

Special consideration and checks have to take place when a group member has a medical condition that needs specialist equipment to be carried, whether on their own person, by the leader, or both.

Group control.

Leader briefing group.

Leadership

Imagine the setting: a military group nearing the end of their week of adventurous training are paddling towards a very well-known tidal feature.

The leader is near the front of the group, positioned beside the person he considers to be most likely to capsize. He quickly checks that everyone is okay with carrying out the plan before he commits to running through the race, going with the flow. As the first paddler reaches the crest of the entry wave, he capsizes and wet exits.

The leader shouts "CAPSIZE" and goes about performing the rescue. With the casualty back in his kayak, the leader lifts his head and looks around — everyone else is in the water, still being flushed through the feature and beyond. Countless minutes pass and eventually everyone is back in their kayak.

Later, sitting in an eddy there is a period of reflection. The leader then says,

"I need to explain to you the difference between information and an instruction."

Being soldiers, and used to following commands, their first reaction was to follow the command-style instruction that they thought had been issued.

LEADER ABILITIES

There are many leadership styles but all leaders have some things in common and there are certain abilities the leader must have in order to be that leader.

Competence – The leader has to be competent and make decisions based on experience and good reasoning, as well as spiritual and moral outlook.

Confidence – The leader must inspire group members by showing confidence in their abilities. They must display calm confidence in all that they do, or attempt to do.

Open-mindedness – A good leader is fair and open-minded enough to listen to the views of others, yet firm if others' opinions appear less suited to the group.

Honesty – Leaders must also be honest – to the group and to themselves.

Creativity – An imaginative leader will be able to create a variety of unique methods to energise and inspire the group.

STYLES OF LEADERSHIP

The following are models used to describe and analyse the way a leader works. In fact most effective leaders will use different styles in different circumstances and shift seamlessly between them.

I often say to groups at the water's edge briefing that there are three rules: Rule 1, *"Smile"*. Rule 2, *"No matter what happens, smile"*. Rule 3, *"If I need to be in charge, you will know it. You will have no doubt as to what I want you to do, how I want you to do it and when."* I know that my leadership style changes when I feel that there is some element of danger, or that the situation is likely to deteriorate if action is not taken immediately. I am aware of sometimes being a bit of a dictator but it is at these times, when the situation is dire, that followers really need to do what they are being told.

Beach briefing.

AUTOCRATIC (OR COMMAND)

This is the sergeant major approach to leading (the one in the story above); there is no room for manoeuvre and the leader is always right. When decisions are made, there is no reference to the others in the group. It can create a climate of fear within the group but is very useful when control and absolute safety is a must.

PARTICIPATIVE

This is a democratic leadership style which requires group members' input, but where the leader retains the responsibility of making the final decision. This style of leading works best when the group members are able to share their knowledge and are skilled sea kayakers. Communication failures are common when group roles are unclear or decisions have to be made in a time-pressured environment. Leading in this participative style will develop better group morale which will, in turn, lead to better decision making.

TRANSFORMATIONAL

This is a behavioural approach to leadership. It can inspire group members to rise above their own self-interest for the benefit of the whole group, generally resulting in performance that exceeds expectations.

The leader makes the group aware of the importance of the task. The leader then delegates suitable tasks to group members and as a result the whole group performs to a higher standard. This focus promotes feelings of worth, competence and relatedness within the whole group.

LAISSEZ-FAIRE

When led in this style, the trained and experienced group members require little to no supervision or feedback in order to succeed. However, this method often leads to conflict when a group decision has to be made.

FOLLOWERS

When there are leaders, there are also followers. Being a good follower is as difficult as being a good leader. It does not, however, mean that a sheep-like approach should be taken. Whereas a leader has many options to use when considering the best way to approach a problem, the follower has to be a bit more restrained in order for the relationship to flourish. It takes time to develop the knowledge that there are times to follow without question, times to question first before following and times to not follow at all. Very often, people who are good leaders are terrible followers, especially as they already have opinions about whatever the proposed plan is.

How can it work? Firstly, the leader is exactly that and if operating successfully in the role, should be aware of, and make use of, other group members' skills and abilities.

Here are some examples. If a group member is medically trained, it makes sense for that person to deal with any first aid or injuries that may need to be taken care of. If there is a ship's radio operator within the group, they should be the person leading with communications, especially in an emergency situation where clear comms with the rescue services are vital. However, it is important that the leader ensures these individuals are happy to fulfil these group roles, before handing them over at the stressful time of an incident. By agreeing group roles before setting out onto the water, misunderstandings are less likely to happen later.

FOLLOWERSHIP QUALITIES

Judgement – this is a tricky concept. To develop good judgement, a follower has to have lived experiences, both good and bad. Followers have to be able to take directions from a leader, but only when those directions are correct. It is possible to take directions that are agreed not to be the best, but if the command is plain wrong, it would be foolish to comply. Someone who shows good judgment as a follower, will make a good leader too.

Work ethic – good followers work hard and are motivated. They commit to the overall group effort, and pay attention to the detail of the situation.

Competence – the follower has to be competent enough to carry out the task allocated by the leader. If something goes wrong because the follower was not competent in the given task, the fault lies with the leader, rather than the follower. A good follower will volunteer for tasks they feel competent to carry out and share their concerns if they do not feel up to the job.

Honesty – if the follower believes that the leader is making the wrong decision, for any reason, it is their duty to openly discuss this with the leader. Obviously, it is important that the follower is polite and acts with respect during the discussion, but it would be a stupid follower who sat back and did nothing while the whole plan unravelled. Bad leaders do not accept feedback of any type, while good leaders will accept any constructive feedback. Good followers give constructive feedback and poor followers give no feedback, merely becoming sheep.

Courage – it takes courage to confront a leader. It is difficult enough to comment on a plan that is failing, but even more so to confront a leader about their method of leading, particularly if that leader is in a senior position within the group, organisation, or better qualified. Sometimes a discreet word with the leader can be enough, while at other times a more open discussion may be necessary.

Selflessness – a follower who has their ego under control is an asset to any group because the goals and performance of the group are more important to them than self-promotion and personal recognition. Working for the better good of the whole group, even when the outcome may not be what the individual follower desires, demonstrates selflessness.

LEADERS NEED FOLLOWERS

While a group is only as good as its leader, it stands that it is also only as good as its followers. Followers will always be in the shadow of the leader, but by being good followers, they are more likely to become better leaders.

BEACH SAFETY BRIEFING

Before setting out as a group, there are many things that need to be thought of, and it is easy to miss something important when the excitement of the day takes over.

A useful mnemonic to ensure everything has been checked is **MYABCDEF**.

Me – an introduction from 'me', the leader, especially if the leader has not paddled with the group previously.

You – short introduction from each group member, including expectations from the day.

Area – the plan for the day including the route, weather and tidal conditions, as well as any hazards or play spots.

Boats and other kit – check all kit and any group safety items, check where they are located. Make sure everyone has food, drink, adequate spare clothing and personal medication.

Communication – agree how the group will communicate, what signals will be used and if a mayday call needs to be made, who will carry it out.

Doctor – a reminder for everyone to carry any medication they may need, and also a gentle nudge for anyone to disclose, privately to the leader, any medical condition that could have an impact on the trip.

Emergency – put in place procedures to be taken in the event of an incident, including who will carry out the rescue and how to manage the expectations of other group members during the incident.

Float plan – confirm that the float plan is accurate and left with the appropriate person. Ensure that the emergency contact knows what to do and when (see *Planning a Trip* chapter).

Crossing to Hirta.

Decision making.

Decision Making

I was leading a six-day expedition around the Isle of Skye. On that day we had already covered about twenty miles, and the wind was increasing from the south-west as we crossed the mouth of Loch Hourn. This was to be our longest crossing and we were fully exposed to the wind. I was paddling alongside John, a client of several years, who didn't look too happy, but was managing well enough. I said to John that Nick was going to capsize within the next ten minutes and that when this happened I would paddle off and perform a rescue. I told John that he was to continue paddling towards Nick and me.

It is no surprise that John wanted to know how I knew this was going to happen. I stumbled my way through an explanation of what I was observing, and how Nick's paddling had changed, which is what had alerted me to the possibility of him capsizing. Nick did fall in, I did rescue him and John did paddle to us both. This incident started me thinking about the process of decision making and, specifically, how we register and analyse the signs or warnings of things starting to go wrong.

Decision making can be either a conscious process, which takes time, or can be almost completely unconscious, relying on what appears to be intuition. It is reasonably well known that the unconscious brain works around twenty times faster than the conscious brain; and it is this that drives the apparently intuitive decision-making process, by using memories of previous incidents, and applying them to the current problem.

It takes a lot of paddling to develop the expertise required for unconscious decision making, an average of ten years or ten thousand hours, according to some research. In the meantime, while we develop this expertise, a crystal ball would be a fantastic possession when it comes to safety and incidents on the sea. Unfortunately, they are hard to come by so instead we have to make do with thinking ahead and being observant.

In this chapter I have set out different decision-making tools to help paddlers at all levels reach decisions for themselves that will have a positive outcome on events.

THINKING AHEAD

By considering a scenario in advance and looking particularly for any flaws in the plan, there is a greater chance of good decisions being made when the situation becomes real. This is almost like carrying out a post mortem before the event.

'Seamanship' is the catch-all word for everything we do relating to sea kayaking: weather monitoring, navigation, safety, maintenance, and the application of the appropriate skill … the list goes on.

Situation Awareness Management (SAM) is a form of applied seamanship. Scenarios are used to think, and work through, specific situations that may occur on a planned journey before the plan is undertaken. If we, as sea kayakers, make the time and effort to think through the possible outcomes of a specific incident, we will increase our likelihood of success if that incident occurs while we are on the water.

SAM allows us to look to the past and evaluate events, accidents or incidents that have already taken place. In the present, it is the constant monitoring of conditions and group members. When looking to the future, we are monitoring conditions, group members, recognising hazards and determining the likely outcome based on previous experiences.

The main focus of this kind of dynamic decision-making process is to look at what is normal. If we know what is normal as a result of our experience, then when something is not normal we are alerted to it, and can respond appropriately to attempt to make the situation normal again.

Time and again I find myself asking the question "What do I do if X happens?". As I travel by myself or with a group on a journey, I am always looking for a way to deal with whatever is likely to happen. If the coastline is vertical the obvious thing is "Where do I land a casualty?". I generally 'see' that someone is about to capsize and tend to know how I am going to carry out the immediate rescue. I am always on the lookout for ways to decrease the severity of the incident by reducing the environmental exposure and think of these reductions as micro escape routes. This really is how Situation Awareness Management is brought to life.

PRACTISING SCENARIOS

We can deliberately speed up our development by analysing past incidents and practising possible future scenarios in a controlled environment. A suitable controlled environment for practising such scenarios would be a safe beach with an onshore wind. The challenge could then be increased by practising on bigger waves or swell. A safe tide race is one where you would drift into slow-moving water, with no chance of being swept out to sea. Knowledge is nothing without understanding and the paddler has to take appropriate steps to develop this understanding.

SAMPLE TRAINING SESSION TO DEVELOP DECISION-MAKING PROCESSES

Here is an example of a session I use quite frequently to allow paddlers to develop decision-making processes; it is not overly complicated but various items can be added which will increase the intensity of the experience. The basis of the incident is a capsized paddler who has exited their kayak and is unconscious. The task is to get the casualty from the water and into a position where the rescue services are able to take them away. The paddlers are initially tasked as a whole group without a specific leader and this can be interesting enough in itself.

The exercise does not need to take place in rough water or an exposed position to start with, as more learning will take place if the group feel safe. I like to choose a sheltered location with very little tidal flow or wind, as this allows time to reflect on the performance and increases the likelihood of a positive outcome. Being close enough to see and hear everything that is going on is good, as it allows me to reflect on where the decisions usually go wrong and then feed this information back to the group.

Generally the first thing any group will try is to lift the person out of the water and onto the decks of the kayaks forming the raft. Although not impossible, this is very difficult and can put all of the rescuers' backs in a weak position increasing the chance of injury. The next thing will be that someone will say to try a scoop rescue. This invariably goes wrong as everyone tries to do something to help, rather than one person taking charge and directing the operation. Normally, the person who is holding the casualty will be the one to take control and they will ask someone else to bring the kayak to them. This is seldom successful and leads to frustration as the kayak always ends up further away from the casualty than it was previously. Around now, someone will suggest calling the coastguard with a mayday broadcast, so everyone will stop to listen, perhaps even offering some information on correct radio protocol. This all leads to a mental overload for everyone involved in attempting to sort out the problem. Frustration follows and communication breaks down with some people opting to sit aside and do nothing.

By reviewing the decision-making process, it is possible to set an order to the proceedings such that a greater chance of success is achieved. The second attempt is inevitably a much smoother operation. A leader is appointed and tasks are allocated. The coastguard is contacted while at the same time the casualty is removed from the water, and other people are preparing a tow.

RULES OF THUMB

Rules of thumb offer a shortcut during times of stressful decision-making. These are simple and efficient rules that are used to shape judgement and make decisions. They are often learnt subconsciously but can be designed and applied consciously. In the story above, the rule of thumb I had taught myself was that when people use shorter strokes and stiffen up,

they are likely to fall in. A capsize is a situation I had dealt with many times in a whole variety of situations. I knew what I was going to do and how I was going to achieve it, even to the point of telling John how he was to behave when it happened.

It is possible however, to introduce bias and error due to previous experiences that could be either good or bad. This often happens when useful guidelines become set in stone. As an example, many paddlers have been told that the leader must never tow, so everything is about making sure that this does not happen, even when it could be the best option. It has become a hard and fast rule for every situation, rather than an advisory statement.

Towing – it's usually a good idea for the leader to get someone else to tow ... but not always.

ASK YOURSELF SOME QUESTIONS

Below are some questions you might ask yourself to allow you to make the best decision when dealing with a developing incident:

Have you seen this before?

Have you seen anything similar to this before?

Have you heard someone else talking about this before?

Have you had to deal with this before?

What did you do?

Did it work?

What was the outcome?

Will it work again?

Will you have to modify it?

When you have answered these questions, you should have a rough plan of what you have to do next to conclude the incident. Better still, ask yourself these questions long before such an incident ever occurs.

"Never put your body where your mind hasn't been." – Chuck Jaeger (test pilot)

CONTEXT OF THE INCIDENT

Decision making takes place in almost everything that is done when going on the water: what to wear, where to go, what to eat, what if ... the list goes on forever, in the context of the activity.

During the timespan of an incident there can be many decisions to make. In an attempt to categorize incidents and neatly arrange them into some sort of framework, I have devised four categories: Simple, Complicated, Complex and Chaotic. These are hierarchical as can be seen in the diagram with 'Simple' involving conscious processes at the bottom and Chaotic at the top corresponding to unconscious thought processes. Below are definitions and examples of the type of incident you may come across.

Context and complexity of incidents.

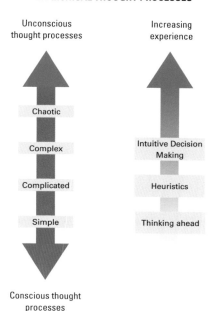

HIERARCHICAL THOUGHT PROCESSES

Unconscious thought processes

Increasing experience

Chaotic

Complex

Intuitive Decision Making

Complicated

Heuristics

Simple

Thinking ahead

Conscious thought processes

A simple rescue.

Simple – This is where everything is known and unlikely to change, everyone involved shares understanding and knowledge of the problem. Often the answer is clear and explicit.

Example – A novice paddler capsizes on flat water due to overbalancing, needs to be rescued and then be put back into their kayak.

Two paddlers needing rescue in rough water close to rocks.

Complicated – Not everyone can see the relationship between the trigger and the outcome and there may be many correct answers. Making decisions in this context takes time and there is a compromise between making decisions quickly and trying to get the right answer.

Example – A paddler capsizes in rough water, close to rocks. Another paddler attempts to perform a rescue but also capsizes, resulting in two people in the water.

Unconscious paddler in water.

Complex – Unfortunately there are no right answers and information is mostly incomplete. Plans will fail if there is an attempt to impose rigid order. Flexibility is required and decisions can only be made as the facts are revealed.

Example – A paddler capsizes and exits their kayak; after this they appear to be unresponsive. They have not banged their head and have no previously disclosed underlying medical condition.

Chaotic – The underlying relationships are in a constant state of flux and there are no obvious patterns that could be used to find an answer. The best option here is to hold off and observe until a pattern emerges. This can help prevent further incidents as well as downgrade the incident from Chaotic to Complex.

Multiple capsizes and group separation.

Example – A group of paddlers has paddled around a headland and conditions are much worse than anticipated. The result is multiple capsizes and separation of some group members from each other as well as from their kayaks and paddles. You hold off until the group is flushed into the calmer water where it becomes clear who has hung onto their equipment and who hasn't. After giving instructions to those with their equipment to swim with their kayak and paddle to the nearest other paddler and get each other back in their kayaks, you concentrate on re-uniting the remaining paddlers with their kayaks.

These categories are only a theoretical model to help us analyse how we have dealt with, or can in the future deal with, incidents. The important thing to realise is that downgrading to the category immediately below the current one, by choosing the action that will have the most beneficial effect on the final outcome, allows better decisions to be made.

GUT FEELINGS

It would be logical to think that the very best decisions are made when there is full access to every detail surrounding the complete incident, and plenty of time to allow this decision to be thought through in its entirety. This is not always the case.

Sometimes, we just have to go with what feels right. These gut feelings are often absolutely spot-on accurate and more so when we have had experience of a similar event happening previously.

CHOOSING NOT TO DO SOMETHING IS ALSO A DECISION

Quite possibly, one of the most difficult decisions is to not do anything to help another person, and the risk is that the memories of standing by will be retained forever. If by making a decision to help someone else, you add yourself to the casualty list, then you are not actually helping in any way. In fact the reverse is true – by doubling the number of casualties you would be lowering the chances of that person being rescued by either the rescue services or another, perhaps more experienced, paddler.

Reading the water.

Reading the Water

It just came at us out of nowhere, a patch of rough water that we had no hope of avoiding. What was it? Where did it come from? Why was it where it was? Perhaps more importantly, how could we have known it was going to appear?

Three of us were paddling around the Isle of Jura on the west coast of Scotland. We were approaching a small headland and we knew what the tides were supposed to be doing, having worked out everything based on the information we could find. The wind was blowing about Force 3 southerly and the tide was running north at about 3 knots. With the wind going the same direction as the tide, the water surface was flat, and as we were going from south to north everything was looking good until we were swept into the unexplained and unantici- pated patch of rough water. Why could we not escape and move to safer water?

Arriving at the headland it started to become more obvious what was going on. The main flow went past the headland with the wind but then an eddy* was forming behind the head- land. The patch of rough water was where the eddy flow met the main current and the wind. This became so obvious when we stopped to think about it, but hadn't been to our inexperi- enced eyes when we were on the water.

*On the sea an eddy can take the form of a large area where the flow is reversed. This is where the sea fills the hole that would otherwise be left when the main flow goes past an obstruction such as a headland. It can be over a distance of many miles! River paddlers often think of eddies as quiet areas where the flow is gently reversed, but on the sea, the eddies can move as fast as the main flow. In river paddling terms, this only happens on really large volume rivers.

I've spent a long time looking at water and observing its patterns, textures and how it moves around and over obstacles since that first unexplained encounter.

NOTICING CHANGES OR DIFFERENCES

As you launch your kayak, you've done your homework; you have a map of the area, you know what the tides are predicted to do, you've checked the latest weather forecast. If you know what is supposed to be happening, you will be better able to interpret any changes.

Now you need to hone your powers of observation. Does the water look the same all around you? Can you spot different patterns and textures? Constantly looking for, and noticing, subtle changes or differences on the surface of the water will help you work out what is going on.

Even if you don't quite understand what is happening, at least you are aware that something is different. This way you won't be caught completely by surprise, and will be in a position to adapt your paddling to the conditions. As you gain experience you will learn to recognise what these patterns indicate.

WHY DO WE WANT TO SEE THE CHANGES?

Forewarned is forearmed. If we can detect any differences sooner, it is possible to react to the developing situation and change what we do to avoid the consequences of a perhaps worsening situation.

If we are in calm water and notice an area of darker water, we may not know what it is that is happening, but we won't be caught by surprise, as we do know that it will be different to where we currently are.

WHAT CAUSES PATTERNS TO APPEAR ON THE WATER?

All the patterns and textures we see on the water are produced by interactions between different forces and elements. The main ones are wind, water, waves, tidal flows, a river flowing into the sea, the shape of the sea bottom, the shape of the land, and isolated rocks above or below the surface.

WHAT PATTERNS AND TEXTURES ARE WE LOOKING FOR?

The interaction of at least two of the factors mentioned above will affect how the water behaves and create a distinctive pattern.

Light / Dark

If you are paddling towards a lighter patch of water it could indicate that the water is shallower or the bottom is sandy. If there is a large swell you may wish to stay in the deeper, darker-coloured water.

A patch of darker water moving towards you may indicate a gust of wind. The wind ruffles the surface of the water, which as a result reflects less light –

The dark lines on the water beyond the paddlers indicates a gust changing the surface reflections.

the darker the surface of the water, the stronger the gust. (Really strong, long-lasting gusts or squalls may appear as a dark line, or a white one if they are strong enough to lift spray off the water.) Be ready to lower your paddles so they don't catch the wind and keep looking to see where the gust will end as the water surface will change again.

Colour

A particularly violent squall passes in the same direction as the paddlers.

Green or turquoise water is usually shallow. Dark blue water is usually deep. A sudden change to muddy brown colour may indicate an outflow of a river in flood. You might want to change course so as to ferry glide across the current, or avoid it by going further out to sea, or even inshore to the confluence and ferry glide there.

Size

The size of the waves is important, even if only to ensure your stories are listened to after the paddle! Waves change size as they move away from where they've been created and drastically increase in height as they approach a beach or headland or a shallower area of the sea.

Shape

The colour of the water shows differences in the bottom and depth.

The shape of waves changes as they encounter different conditions. If the wind and tide are flowing in the same direction, then the waves will be smaller and more spaced out. When the flow changes direction, the waves will increase in size and the face away from the wind will steepen and start to break. Waves also change shape and usually steepen as they approach a beach or other shallow area. Sometimes the change is quite subtle and at other times it is fairly obvious.

WIND AND WAVES

Having looked at the big picture, let's now look in more detail at these pattern makers.

Waves are formed by wind and changed by the wind, tidal flow and the shape of the land. Let's start with how waves are formed.

DEEP WATER WAVES OR SWELL

The wind acting on the surface of the water develops waves and the greater the distance over which the wind blows, the bigger the swell becomes. This distance is known as the fetch.

Swell is often formed a long way out in the ocean, so the waves you see are often not travelling in the same direction as the local wind.

A FULLY DEVELOPED SEA

If the fetch is long enough, a 'fully developed sea' will occur. This happens when the waves are travelling at close to the speed of the wind and the wind is no longer able to transfer any energy to the waves, so the sea state reaches its maximum (for that wind speed).

The fetch required for a fully developed sea increases relative to the strength of the wind, and the table below gives an indication of what length is needed to build the wave height stated. It is worth noting that even if the fetch is longer than the distance at which the waves obtain their maximum height, the swell cannot increase further unless the wind increases.

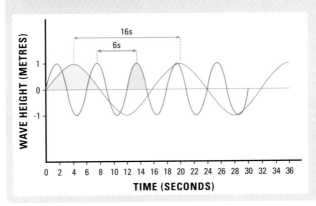

Wave height and swell period as it relates to the volume of water and therefore energy contained in a wave.

FULLY DEVELOPED SEA WIND, FETCH AND WAVE DETAIL					
WIND			**AVERAGE WAVE**		
Force / speed of wind in one direction in knots	Fetch in nautical miles	Duration in hours	Height in metres	Wavelength in metres	Period in seconds
Force 3 10kn	10	2	0.3m	8m	3
Force 5 20kn	75	10	1.5m	34m	6
Force 7 30kn	280	25	4m	77m	8.5
Force 8 40kn	710	45	8.5m	136m	11
Force 10 50kn	1420	70	15m	212m	14

Table showing the wind conditions required for a fully developed sea and the specifics of the waves developed.

A good way to work out how much power there is in a given wave is to count the time (period) in seconds that it takes from crest to crest, for one complete wave to pass. This time can vary from as little as one second to 30 seconds and sometimes more. A one metre swell at 20 seconds contains substantially more volume of water than a one metre swell at 8 seconds.

WIND (LOCAL) WAVES

Wind waves are very different to swell waves. Local wind-generated waves have little power compared to distant wind-generated swell. They tend to go in the same direction as the wind and are smaller and steeper than ocean swell.

Wind waves travelling in a different direction to the swell often make for a confused and messy sea. On the water, you will often see waves coming from different directions.

Sometimes, when there is a large swell running, there can be a cross swell as well as local wind-generated waves, all coming together. As you can imagine, when the peaks of these three different waves meet, the result can feel like being in an elevator, going up one moment and then rapidly down the next. It is an uncomfortable sea to journey in, and both mentally and physically demanding.

HOW LAND SHAPE AFFECTS WIND AND WAVES

Land, and its particular shape, changes the way the wind and the waves behave. Their un-impeded race across the ocean is suddenly curtailed as they meet a landmass.

REFLECTED WAVES

When waves meet a vertical shore profile, the energy rebounds. Sometimes, part of the energy is absorbed by the shore and the reflected wave doesn't have quite the same power as the initial wave, instead it nearly doubles in height and steepness. Reflected waves are often described as a 'confused' sea, and kayakers know this as 'clapotis'.

Reflected waves off a vertical section of coast.

Exactly how a reflected wave will behave will depend on many things, but if the waves are bigger, the reflected waves will be bigger too. On a stretch of coastline it is possible to get haystack waves, reflected walls of waves, as well as other interference patterns, all de-pending on the angle of the vertical rock face. If the waves are entering a channel between vertical rock and an island, the sea becomes completely chaotic as in the image below.

Reflected waves between Hirta and Mina Stac on St Kilda.

REFRACTION

Where there is an obstruction, such as an island, a headland, or a harbour wall, the swell will often wrap around it; this is called 'refraction' and allows waves to reach places where they are not expected. On the sheltered side of an island there will most likely be a wave 'shadow', where there are no waves whatsoever, but a little further out, approximately the width of the island away, there will be interference and a doubling of the wave energy.

Around a headland, the swell behaves slightly differently. As headlands usually continue underwater, the sea is shallower and the waves start to gently refract before they reach the headland. This causes the waves to slow down, increase in size, and steepen. The waves are largest off the end of a headland.

Once past the headland, the wave will decrease in size and follow the shape of the land until it meets some other obstruction where it will change again.

The direction of the swell relative to coastal features will determine where the biggest waves will form and where the most sheltered places will be. The largest waves will form off a headland, and the next largest where the land faces directly towards the swell direction. The smallest waves will appear at 180º to the swell, as the diagram overleaf shows, and are approximately 10% of the size of the largest waves.

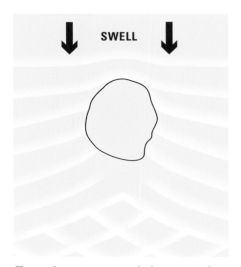

The interference pattern created when a wave refracts around an obstacle and collides with itself.

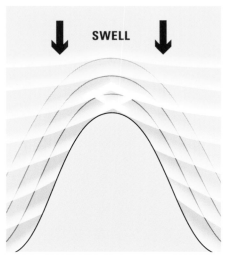

As the swell approaches a headland, the waves start to 'feel' the bottom, gently refract and steepen. All of the energy in the ocean is focused in the immediate vicinity offshore of the headland.

It can be difficult to see exactly what is happening within the confused water, especially when the coastline is irregular. Each section that is reflecting wave energy does so at a different angle. This makes reading the water more difficult as there is a less defined pattern to the wave shape.

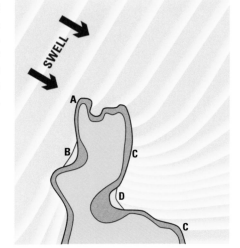

Size of swell relative to swell direction, how much it refracts and reduces in size.
A = 3m
B = 3m + surf
C = 50%
D = 10%

NARROWING

When there is a narrowing of a channel, many things happen. The first is that the wind speed generally increases and the water appears to be flowing. The kayak will be pushed along more swiftly as a result, and the waves will most likely increase in height.

If the narrowing is sudden, there will be an area of interference at the entrance to the narrows; this is due to the wave's energy rebounding off the rocks on either side of the channel. This patch of 'funny' water will look much like haystacks, small peaks of waves surrounded on all sides by deep troughs.

The change in surface area from the open water to the channel has an impact on how far the waves penetrate into the channel. Refraction will be occurring on both sides of the channel due to the friction between the water and the land. Often, the easiest place to get through these conditions is close to either side where the waves are most likely to be smaller and less powerful.

WIDENING

When the wind and waves move through a narrow channel that opens up to a wider area, the waves tend to become diffused and refract towards the land on either side. In the middle of the channel, the waves continue in their original direction of travel.

HAYSTACK WAVES

Haystack waves can be intimidating, as one second you can be completely surrounded by water, when you're in the trough, and the next you can be up in the air on the crest of one of the peaks with no water at all around you.

The same thing can happen when the waves are reflecting off the face of a cliff and heading straight back out towards the next incoming wave, though the explosion of water when both waves collide is much more powerful.

TURNING A KAYAK IN HAYSTACK WAVES

Turning in haystack waves can be difficult. You may be tempted to try the manoeuvre in the trough as it will feel more stable. However, both the bow and stern of the kayak will be in the water and it will be difficult to make even slight changes in direction.

By attempting the turn on the top of the wave, less of the kayak will be affected by the water, and there is the comforting knowledge that there will be plenty of water when you descend into the trough.

A very big reflected wave. Photo: Jason Davis

ROCKS AND ISLANDS

Whenever there is a rock, island or even an iceberg in the path of the waves, they behave in a predictable manner. Firstly, the waves slow down as they meet the obstruction, then they begin to wrap around it. If the approach is steep, there will be reflected waves.

Waves refracted around an iceberg.

Behind the obstruction there will be a wave shadow, a place where there are almost no waves. Away from the shore, things will get a bit more exciting with waves coming from both sides and making a very confused interference pattern. This will be most pronounced approximately the width of the island away, with tall haystack waves and steep, deep troughs.

If the bottom is sand in the lee of the land, then there will be a slightly different wave pattern. As the waves wrap around the island, the area where the wave shadow should be will be filled with sand, creating a spit offshore. Where the spit interrupts the wave action, a great deal of vertical energy will follow the line of the spit directly away from the island. The wave formed behaves a bit like a zipper in that it runs away from where the two colliding swells first meet.

Vertical energy as a result of refraction around a rock. Photo: Mark Boyd

ROUND VERSUS ANGULAR

A rounded rock will allow the waves to follow the shape of the rock more than if the rock had a sharper angle. This is due to refraction and friction; the waves refract around the contour, but when there is a sharp departure from the general direction, the wave becomes separated from the rock. This results in a safer area behind an angular rock with less energy being expended than behind a smooth, rounded rock.

SHELF

A rock shelf can be an intimidating feature as the waves seem to suck dry from the top and then crash over it. As the swell approaches the rock, the water level drops, and runs off the rock towards the direction of the incoming swell. This creates a 'stopper' (hydraulic), which fills as the swell comes in. These are similar to those found on a river, with one major difference; a 'hydraulic' created by a wave or swell will dissipate quickly, releasing the paddler from its clutches, whereas a river feature will keep hold for a long time.

ISOLATED REEF

A shallow area, such as a reef, will cause swell and waves to break, often more suddenly and violently than a gradual shallowing of the water. Often these will appear as 'boomers' where the energy of the wave is converted to noise in one quick boom, as the name suggests. The sneaky thing about boomers is that they may appear as a slight steepening of the wave as it passes over a submerged reef, until a particularly big set of waves comes in, at which point they will break over the reef.

A paddler dropping into a large hydraulic on the California coast. Photo: Mark Boyd

A boomer appearing inshore of a group paddling in swell.

CLOSE TO THE ROCKS

FOLLOW THE DARK WATER

The colour of the water is important when close to rocks and other obstructions. Dark water is normally only moving up and down, whereas light-coloured (aerated) water is flowing somewhere. This could be forwards, back, up, down, sideways or in all directions at once. In white, aerated water a kayak will have less buoyancy, and it will be harder to get decent purchase with the paddle than in dark non-aerated water. The size of the white water area indicates how much the kayak is likely to be affected by the water.

This interface between water and rock is where many people choose to play in their kayaks, often not understanding what is going on in the hydraulic maelstrom. A better place to start would be where the rock is near vertical as the interface zone is always narrow. Watching seals in this location is great as they move up and down in time with the water, appearing to do nothing except relax. They never seem to hit the rock and always find the best place to be.

Narrow interface next to almost-vertical rock. Photo: Michaela MacDonald

A wide interface suggests a less than vertical slope, and the bigger the area, the more violent the action of the water becomes. Often the water runs in and out of a gully on a stretch of vertical rock, creating an area of considerable flow, both in and out. When this happens there is often a white patch within the dark water where the air is trapped, making it easier to see the direction and speed of the flowing water. The bubbles trapped in the water move in the direction the white water is moving. This will take the kayak and turn it either towards or away from the gully.

Wide interface formed where there are shallows, the white water is flowing. Photo (R): Michaela MacDonald

Following a dark line to ensure the safest route between obstacles. Photo: Michaela MacDonald

When looking for the safest line between areas of turbulence, the dark line shows the way. Acting almost as a roadmap through the white water, it shows where the areas of least turbulence are. Any places where there are slashes of white across the dark line indicate a spot where your kayak will be pushed to the side. Generally, this dark line is the absolutely safest place to be when among rocks and swell. It is also a good place to perform a rescue if the need should arise.

FRIENDLY FOAM

A place where foam gathers on the surface of the water is generally very safe. This is usually where a null point occurs (the cancelling out of forces). As there is so little movement, everything gathers, and as well as foam, you will find lots of weed and general rubbish. Everything quietens when sitting among the foam.

Looking down from a cliff top, it is possible to work out where there will be less movement on the surface, just by identifying where the foam lies.

Foam on the surface indicates a safe place to paddle.

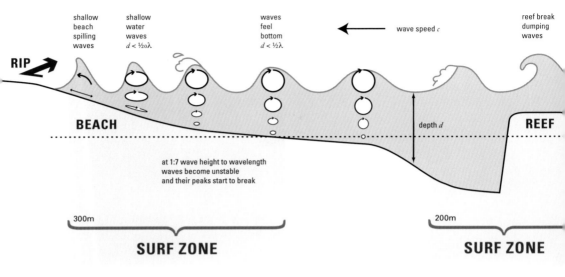

shallow beach spilling waves

shallow water waves $d < \frac{1}{20}\lambda$

waves feel bottom $d < \frac{1}{2}\lambda$

wave speed c

reef break dumping waves

RIP

BEACH

REEF

depth d

at 1:7 wave height to wavelength waves become unstable and their peaks start to break

300m

200m

SURF ZONE

SURF ZONE

SURF

What happens as a wave approaches a beach?

When the depth of the water is half the length of the wave, the wave starts to change. The waves slow down, the wavelength shortens but the period (the time from one crest to the next) remains constant. This causes the waves to change shape; the crests become shorter but the troughs get longer. The waves continue to become steeper, and break when the depth becomes less than 1.3 times the height.

WAVE ENERGY

Waves on water store the energy imparted by the wind that caused them, and this energy is dissipated when it reaches land.

Like other types of wave, the energy is proportional to the square of its height. This means that a 2 metre high wave has 2 x 2 = 4 times the energy of a 1 metre high wave and so on.

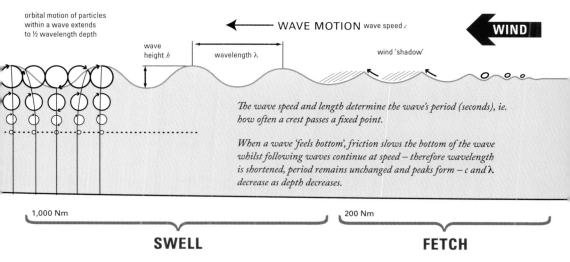

orbital motion of particles
within a wave extends
to ½ wavelength depth

← WAVE MOTION wave speed c

WIND

wave
height b · wavelength λ

wind 'shadow'

*The wave speed and length determine the wave's period (seconds), ie.
how often a crest passes a fixed point.*

*When a wave 'feels bottom', friction slows the bottom of the wave
whilst following waves continue at speed – therefore wavelength
is shortened, period remains unchanged and peaks form – c and λ
decrease as depth decreases.*

1,000 Nm   200 Nm

SWELL   FETCH

Formation of swell and how surf forms.

When a wave breaks, the energy that is contained within it is transformed into noise and some heat. There is more energy converted if the slope of the land is gentle. The steeper the slope of the land, the more the energy is reflected back to sea to continue its journey until it either decays or connects with a piece of land.

The manner in which surf breaks is determined by the shape of the seabed or shore.

SPILLING WAVES

These are the classic waves we see on a gently sloping sandy beach. The energy contained in the wave is released gradually giving a characteristic breaking white top that makes its way towards the shore, sometimes reforming and breaking again.

A spilling wave travelling towards the shore.

RIPS

A gently sloping beach will produce spilling waves. These are present whenever rows of breakers are rolling towards the beach. Each wave arriving onto a beach brings water with it, and somewhere along the beach the accumulated water has to flow back out to sea, away from the beach. This is known as a rip.

By identifying the rip, it is possible to launch through reasonable-sized surf and use the power of the rip to get out safely.

Rips can move at up to four knots, so if you capsize in a rip, attempting to swim to shore against the flow is not a great idea. It is much better to swim parallel to the beach until you are no longer in the rip, and then use the larger waves that are travelling towards the shore to help carry you in.

If a river enters the sea, there is likely to be a feature similar to a rip, but this time the flow is the river current. When the waves meet this flow, there can often be conditions similar to overfalls or standing waves. Anything caught in the flow will go out to sea.

A key skill is the ability to predict where the rip is likely to form and then to identify it. The most obvious place for the rip to occur is at the opposite end of the beach from the swell direction. The rip will appear as a flattened area of water running out to sea, along rocks if there are any. The waves here will be smaller than those on either side of the rip and may not even be breaking at all. The outgoing water gets its energy from the incoming water; this means that the bigger the waves breaking on the beach, the stronger the rip will be.

REFRACTED SURF

When waves meet a gently sloping beach at an angle, the effect is as mentioned above. The wave slows down, changes and then starts to break. Because of the angle, some parts of the wave are still in deeper water and haven't broken yet. The effect we see is a breaking wave travelling along the beach, always bending towards the land.

A wave bending towards the land due to refraction.

Sometimes the rip will form where a stream or river enters the bay. This rip will be stronger than if it was only caused by the waves, as it will have the volume of the river going out to sea as well.

On a very long beach, rips will form at intervals when the pressure of the water dictates. Taking a look at low water will guide you to the location of the rip because there will be water covering the sand. The deepest channel at low water is where the rip forms.

A typical rip forming at the right-hand end of the beach, close to rocks.

DUMPING WAVES

These waves occur when the beach is very steep. The process is that the waves coming from deeper water, suddenly 'feel' the bottom. They steepen very quickly and collapse suddenly. The energy is quickly expended in one explosive crash and is often amplified by the outgoing backwash of the previous wave.

A dumping wave expending most of its energy.

These beaches are often steep with soft sand or fine shingle that does not provide a good stable base when trying to stand. Often, waiting for a group of lower waves, or 'lull', is a suitable option for getting afloat or ashore.

Dumping waves are easily recognised from the shore but not so obvious from the sea. Be particularly wary when approaching a beach where there is a large swell but you cannot see the waves breaking. These waves are very powerful and can break boats.

The power of a dumping wave should not be underestimated. Here it launches a loaded kayak into the air.

SURGING WAVES

These waves run up the shore producing large surges of water and often, lots of foam. This is not a nice type of wave as the power in it, added to the volume of water moving around, makes it difficult to control anything. There is a high chance that you and your kayak will be dragged over the rocks that are guaranteed to be there.

A surging wave pushing water all the way to the top of the beach – waiting for the right time to launch is crucial.

DIFFERENCES AT HIGH OR LOW WATER

A change in the height of the tide will bring about a change in what is exposed and what is covered. Often a beach looks completely different at low water when compared to high. Springs and neaps will have a similar effect.

Obstructions that are unseen when covered at high water can become boat-breaking rocks when the tide drops enough. The profile of the beach can also change as the tide rises and falls. A beach that has a gentle angle and gently spilling waves at low water may have a steep angle and dangerous dumping waves at high water.

FLOW (TIDAL STREAMS)

Much has been written about tidal flows, especially about the Rule of Thirds and the 50 / 90 Rule. These give a speed of flow at a specific time in the tidal cycle, and for more information and how to work out speeds and timings, I refer you to *Sea Kayak Navigation* by Franco Ferrero (Pesda Press).

When a body of water is flowing and meets an obstruction it behaves in a consistent way. The volume of water and its speed will determine how the feature will develop. Understanding how the water moves and behaves around a feature will allow you to read the water and work out the best line to take.

Unlike a river, which remains pretty constant, the flow on the sea is constantly, but predictably, changing. After a short period of slack water, the flow starts slowly and builds towards maximum speed before slowing and then, after a short period of slack water, changing direction.

As the tide goes towards high water, there will be more water covering the rocks. The reverse is also true as low water is approached. At low water, there will be less water and possibly more weed to deal with.

Any narrowing, or shallowing, of a channel will result in a speeding up of the flow. Any widening or deepening will result in a decreased flow.

The flow will increase in speed and change direction immediately next to an obstruction and several things can happen.

SEE THE WATER FLOW ...

In a narrow channel where the tidal stream flows as fast as a powerful river, it's easy to see the water moving. However, when the movement is slower, the channel wider, or you are on the open sea, it is not so obvious. With a great deal of practice you will be able to tell that the water is moving in a certain direction, because the waves are steeper, or flatter, than they should be, given the wind conditions. Meanwhile, until you 'get your eye in' you will need some indicators or clues:

Boats at anchor or on a mooring buoy will usually point into the tide, unless the tide is very weak or the wind is much stronger and having a greater effect.

Any obstruction in the flow will have a 'cushion wave' upstream, the flow forming a V shape, and an eddy immediately downstream (zone of water where the flow is reversed). These obstructions might be a buoy, a perch (pole used instead of a buoy to mark a channel), or a rock (see below for more detail).

Anchored boat pointing into the tide.

Obstruction in the flow causing a V shape and eddy.

Obstruction in the flow causing a cushion wave.

MUSHROOMS OR BOILS

Mushroom patterns or boils on the surface indicate an upwelling of water from the seabed. The water movement in these is from the centre outwards and if you paddle through one, your kayak will be pushed out to the side of the mushroom.

Conical buoy leaning downstream, away from the flow.

Buoys lean away from the flow (not so easy to see with round buoys).

Look for floating objects to see which way they are moving. Bear in mind that the wind may be having more effect than the tide, unless more of the object is under the water than above the surface. Unattached seaweed is a good indicator, a beach ball is a bad one.

If you are afloat and close to the shore, you will be able to see which way you are moving in relation to stationary objects on the shore. If you are further out, it is not at all obvious and you will need to use transits to work out which way the flow (or the wind) is taking you. This involves finding a distant and a nearby object that line up with you. If they become unaligned you are moving.

Photos 1–3: Using Stac Lee and Stac an Armin as a transit to detect drift. Stac an Armin is beyond Stac Lee and the drift is to the right over the three images.

The skill here is not to fight it but allow the flow to take you away from your intended track while at the same time keeping an overview of where you are heading. As long as your general direction is maintained, progress over the ground will be quicker. If there are many mushrooms close together, your kayak will be nudged from side to side as it bounces from

The smooth water of a mushroom pushes the kayak to the left and the rougher water can be seen clearly around the mushroom.

one to the next. Between the mushrooms there will be areas of slightly rougher water and these indicate where the two, or more, flows meet and produce interference. Your kayak will behave more predictably here, following the line between the mushrooms.

EDDIES

An eddy will form behind an obstruction – here the water flows in the opposite direction to the main stream. This can be on a small scale, e.g. an eddy a few metres long behind a small rock, or on a large scale, such as an eddy behind a major headland several miles long. There can be additional eddies inside a main eddy and each one will flow in the opposite direction to the previous one.

CUSHION WAVES

The water level on the upstream side of an obstruction will be higher than that on the downstream side; sometimes this difference in height can be quite considerable. This is called a cushion wave. The flow here will be along the upstream face before turning and running past the obstruction. This cushion wave can be a good place to paddle when going upstream, as the water is not really moving very quickly, but care needs to be taken to ensure you don't connect with the rock.

CLIMBING OVER THE WALL

The main eddy normally flows at a similar rate to the main flow. This results in a differential in speed, twice that of the calculated flow. This means that in powerful flows, at the top of the eddy, there will be an 'eddy wall' where the two opposing currents meet. You will actually be able to see a water level difference. Sometimes it can be difficult to get over this 'wall' into the eddy.

Some eddies can be several miles long while others are more like those found on a river.
Photo (L): Ken Nicol

At my local tide race I've sat in the eddy below where the water hits the rock and the water was at eye level. The eddy wall here is a 45cm step and with the water flowing at eight knots it is more than just a bit intimidating. Obviously, this is a fairly unusual situation and does not happen everywhere.

Looking upstream from the eddy behind rocks with the water at eye level.

SURFACE EDDIES

Irregularities on the seabed will often show on the surface. An obstruction some way below the water surface can produce a surface eddy, this is normally a good place to rest as you paddle upstream against the flow. Being able to see these features while paddling is a great skill to develop. To identify a surface eddy, look for very small standing waves downstream of an area where there is disturbed water, and for the obvious movement of water back upstream.

A surface eddy caused by an obstruction well below the water surface.

ROCK LEDGES IN THE FLOW

As the level of the water rises, a rock ledge will form a stopper or hydraulic, much the same as found on rivers. This soon fills and becomes a wave, before washing out completely. The reverse happens as the tide drops, a flat stretch of water will change to a wave, then a stopper, before becoming a rock in the stream again. Unlike on a river, this type of feature does not stay constant; as the direction, height and speed of the flow change, so too does the feature.

A stopper formed when the water flows over a ledge.

FLOW MEETING FLOW

Different flows meeting result in some very funny confused water; sometimes one flow rides over the other and at other times it flows below. As a general rule, the water in the immediate vicinity of the meeting point will be flowing almost vertically downwards. By manoeuvring into a position where you can observe what is happening, you will be able to determine how the water is actually flowing.

The water in the image is flowing from bottom left and from middle right converging in the middle. Eddies can be clearly seen on the left behind the headland.

FLOW AGAINST SWELL

When the swell meets with the flow and the two are opposing, some interesting things start to happen. The size of the waves will increase and the space between them will decrease, the tops will collapse on the side facing towards the flow. A similar effect occurs when a river opens out into the sea.

Opposing swell and flow creating breaking waves.

Strong wind against the flow creates a lot of small, closely-spaced breaking waves.

EFFECTS OF WIND ON TIDAL FLOW

Wind against tide has the same effect as flow against swell but the waves produced are generally smaller.

Wind with tide, when the direction of the wind is the same as the direction of the flow, will cause any waves to reduce in size and flatten out.

The surrounding topography may change the general wind direction, with the result that there could be wind against tide conditions where not expected. This is especially likely in a narrow-sided fjord and behind an island.

A strong wind across a tidal flow produces haystack waves that travel downstream.

If there are hills on either side, then consider the likelihood of there being downdraughts that will blow across the flow, possibly causing some funny water. This can take the form of haystack waves travelling downstream and is generally most noticeable on the eddy lines.

ALWAYS TRY TO KEEP AN EYE ON THE BIG PICTURE

When I look at a chart, I try to bring everything into a perspective I can easily understand. Instead of an island, I imagine a rock in a stream. Instead of overfalls forming off a headland, I imagine what the land looks like below the water. Instead of an eddy, I imagine a magic carpet ride to get me upstream. By attempting to simplify the movement of water as it flows into, over, around or through an obstacle, whether it is a rock, an island or a headland, I am able to build a much better picture of what will actually be happening once I am at the location.

WEIRD THINGS CAN HAPPEN

Our brain can play some spectacular tricks on us. There is one that often happens with flow. Everything has to be lined-up and straight sided for us to make sense of it, so our unconscious mind does this automatically. If you see a bridge going across a channel, the land on each side seems to be aligned at right angles to the bridge whether it is or not.

As a result of all the brain-induced interference, it can be difficult to really see what is going on. So for example it can be very difficult to cross the flow at a fine enough angle for a ferry glide, because your brain is lying to you about the angle at which the water is flowing.

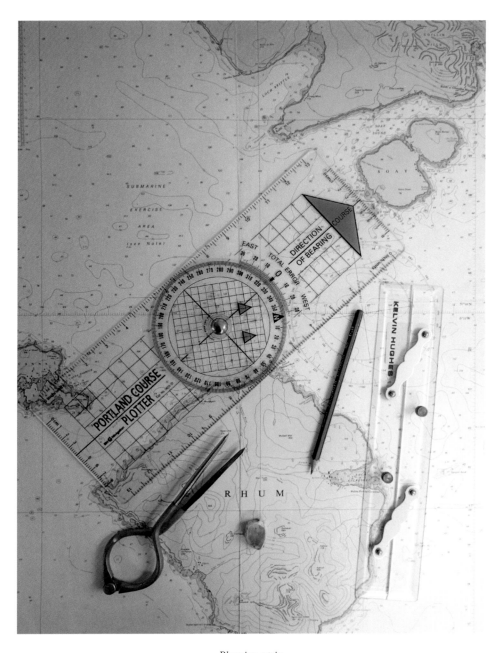

Planning a trip.

Planning a Trip

I remember sitting at home, planning my first 'real' trip. I had the pilot book in front of me, as well as the chart and a set of tide tables. I had been taught how to work out tidal heights, flow direction and speed, and attempted to apply this to the information that was now in front of me.

I failed miserably. Nothing that I planned worked out. Not one of the timings was correct. The flow was not going in the direction I had calculated, nor was it going at the speed I had estimated. I was completely overloaded with information and didn't know how to narrow it down to give me the detail that I needed. I didn't die however, and learned many lessons in planning which I now apply every time I plan a trip. Many years later, I realised that I had been taught using a set of ideals as opposed to real information.

Planning a trip takes many forms and a lot depends on who is going, and when and where they are preparing to go. Much of the planning can be carried out well in advance, especially as far as route selection goes. Charts and maps of a suitable quality are available for pretty much everywhere you would be likely to paddle, as is tidal information. Sea kayaking guide books are also a good source of information and inspiration for your own adventures.

BEFORE THE TRIP

Planning is an important, integral part of a trip and can be an enjoyable part of the experience in itself. Any planning practice that you undertake should use real data from real sources, and if you plan day trips in the future, you will be able to paddle them and check your planning against the actual conditions you encounter. Make notes in your pilot book or guidebook, especially where your observations differ from what is written, so that if you return to that area you will have a better understanding of how the tides work.

GROUP

The first thing to consider is the group; how many people are going, what is their skill level and ability, how far are they able to paddle each day, do they all get along, are there any wildcards or unknowns within the group? These are all questions that need to be answered during the initial stages.

For some paddlers, seven or eight nautical miles a day is enough, but there are others who are not happy unless they are covering 20 miles each day. If you are undertaking a multi-day journey remember to build in some 'rest' days, these are not necessarily days of rest but more contingency days. They ensure that if the weather is poor, or there is some other issue slowing the progress of the group, you will still be able to reach your destination.

EXPECTATIONS

Group, as well as individual, expectations have to be taken into account and should be as closely aligned as possible. If one group member's expectation is that they will be paddling every day and covering at least 30 nautical miles, it might not fit too well with the others who plan on paddling 15 miles a day and having a rest day for every four paddling days.

ROUTE

The route choice, distance to be paddled, conditions that are likely to be encountered and number of days, will depend on the group as much as the time available. When looking at the chart or map together with your proposed route, make a note of any known or potential landing places, paying particular attention to any roads that come close enough to allow the trip to be shortened if the weather conditions deteriorate. If you plan on doing a there-and-back route, take into account the prevailing conditions, so that you get an easier ride back to your start point when you are tired.

A good beginners' trip would be something in the region of 10 to 15 miles with available landing places every mile or so, no areas of big swell, reflected waves or tide races, and a fair wind assisting but not building up a following sea. As soon as these baselines start to change, the journey becomes more committing. A much more advanced trip would be between 20 and 30 miles, continuous exposure to swell and reflected waves, no easy landing areas or at least no landings for considerable periods of time. Breaking waves, tide races, big headlands and open crossings would all add to the seriousness of the journey.

TIDES AND TIDAL STREAMS (FLOWS)

These can be predicted in advance, and time can be taken during the planning phase to ensure that everyone involved understands what is likely to be happening, at what time and how strong. *Sea Kayak Navigation* by Franco Ferrero (Pesda Press) is a good book to help with tidal and more specific trip planning detail.

As a general principle, you will want any tidal movement to be running in your favour. On a one-way trip, and as a general rule, you will have approximately six hours of assistance. To extend this, start paddling one hour before slack against the flow, it will already have slowed down considerably. You will then enjoy the whole of the slack period and the full six hours of flow in your direction. You can continue for an hour after slack as the flow turns against your direction of travel, giving you in all approximately eight hours with assistance or minimum hindrance.

When planning a there-and-back trip, aim to arrive at your destination at slack water; this means that you will have the flow with you both ways, assuming your planning is correct. If there is a tide race, which you want to avoid, ensure you don't arrive in the middle two hours of the flow. If you want to play in the race, then these two hours will give you best sport.

WEATHER

The weather is normally the last thing to be checked as the departure date draws closer, but it is worth finding out about the prevailing weather conditions for the area you are planning to go to, as well as seeking out local advice about any peculiarities.

Apart from lightning (covered below), wind will have the greatest effect on your plans as it can blow you before it or hold you back, in equal measure. Generally speaking, winds of up to Force 3 in places where there are opportunities to gain shelter, are suitable for novice to intermediate paddlers.

Force 3 to Force 5 is definitely the top wind strength for intermediate paddlers and most advanced paddlers will start to feel twitchy. Anything above Force 5 is advanced paddling, and anyone venturing onto the sea in these conditions must be self-sufficient in all areas of their performance. If the wind is offshore and strong, care should be taken to minimise the offshore drift, if something were to happen.

If lightning is forecast, I strongly recommend not going onto the water. If you hear thunder when on the water, you are close enough to the storm to be struck by lightning, so get to land as quickly as possible. Don't seek shelter below a cliff or in a cave as the electric charge may bridge the gap at the narrowest point; this will most likely be the top of your head.

Forecasts are fairly reliable these days but a safe bet is to make a decision the night before, then confirm in the morning, just before leaving.

EQUIPMENT

Consider using a checklist to ensure everyone has all the right equipment.

If you are the leader, are you the only one with a first aid kit and tow system? If the answer is yes, ask your group this question – "*Who does first aid on the first aider?*".

I recommend that everyone in the group carries a towline and that there is a set of spare paddles between each group of three.

Is the camping equipment fit for purpose? It is no use finding out on the night it is first put up, that the tent one of the group is using for a month-long trip in Greenland is a twenty year old festival tent with tie up door flaps (this happened to me).

Are stoves and fuel bottles compatible? Does everyone have enough food of the right type to last for the duration of the trip, plus a few days extra (just in case of contingencies)?

CONTINGENCIES

Planning for the 'what if' scenario is always beneficial. This could be as simple as making sure that you have charts for adjacent areas if plans have to change due to weather conditions.

ON THE DAY

Some things are best left until the day of the trip.

FLOAT PLAN

Leaving a float plan with a responsible shore-based contact is beneficial, as they will be able to initiate a rescue if you are long overdue and have not contacted them to inform them of your changed plans. Your float plan can be prepared and left beforehand, but it will need to be updated if somebody doesn't turn up or the latest weather forecast forces a change of route.

Your float plan should include:

- ◎ Your name and contact details including mobile phone number
- ◎ Total number in the group and total number of kayaks
- ◎ All group members' names, home contact details and any medical considerations
- ◎ The proposed route and any escape routes including specific positions of key places such as campsites or road-accessible landings
- ◎ The location of any parked vehicles, along with the type, colour and registration number, and whether or not there is a trailer
- ◎ Call signs of group members with VHF radios and whether anyone is carrying a PLB (Personal Location Beacon) and / or flares
- ◎ Expected time to be ashore with the trip completed
- ◎ Action to be taken if no contact has taken place within a given time.

ROLES AND RESPONSIBILITIES

Every person in the group needs to know who is taking on what responsibility and what the group expects of them. This is best covered in a beach briefing before you get on the water. (See *Paddling in a Group* and *Leadership* chapters.)

RESCUES

It is worth deciding in advance the roles that every group member is going to play in the event of any rescues having to be performed. By knowing who is going to do what, much time can be saved if something untoward actually occurs. This is probably best covered in a briefing just before you get on the water.

ESCAPE ROUTES

Having options if the weather conditions deteriorate severely is always a good plan. Sometimes it can be as simple as going inside an island instead of paddling on the outside; at other times it could be a complete turnaround and retracing your paddle strokes back to the start point and then doing something completely different. Although you can identify landing points well in advance, your tactics will have to be decided on the day, taking into account actual weather conditions.

FLEXIBILITY

Your plan has to be flexible enough to withstand changes and still be recognised as a plan.

There are two comments I like about planning, these are:

"*No plan survives first contact with the enemy.*" In a sea kayaking context this means that no matter how much effort you have put into the planning process, the weather or tidal conditions will conspire against you to force you to change the plan.

"*Plan the paddle but don't paddle the plan.*" By keeping an open, flexible approach to the plan when on the water, it is possible to adapt to the changing conditions.

Quite often things start going wrong before you even get to the water, and the most difficult time to stop any plan from going ahead is when everyone is standing on the beach, dressed for action, and just about to get into their kayaks. It requires strength of character to ask everyone to put their kayaks back on the roof rack and change location.

WRAPPING IT UP

Reflecting on the effectiveness of the plan and the trip as a whole is always a very useful exercise, and one that allows everyone to be aware of how things went right and also where things didn't go quite so well. This is especially useful if there was an incident and learning points arise. This is best carried out immediately after the trip. If there have been any learning points, these should be revisited a few weeks later, as this allows for more reflection and forward planning for the next outing.

About to run a pour-over. Photo: Michaela MacDonald

Pour-over.

Rock Hopping

I had negotiated the pour-over successfully and John was coming right behind me, so I moved to a position where I could watch and encourage but stay safe myself. John lined up and waited for big swell to come. When it did he paddled forward but lacked some commitment and as a result slid into the trough in front of the next wave, which of course, was bigger than the last one. Lacking in forward speed he was sucked backwards into the foaming jaws of the next wave, picked up and unceremoniously dumped on top of the rock. With no forward speed as the wave disappeared from below his kayak, he ended up sitting on top of the rock, still in his boat.

The next wave was approaching and if he could manage to get two or three good powerful strokes in, he could move with the water and start to get clear of the rock. If he only managed one stroke, he would end up back in the foaming pit.

Three would have been ideal, but two strokes were all that John managed. He was now being washed from side to side on top of the rock, sometimes the right way up and sometimes not. I would be in a position to help once everything settled down, but was not prepared to go into the maelstrom when there was the chance of his kayak hitting me. John kept rolling and getting into a position where he could paddle off but each time he was hit by the next wave. Finally, Neptune decided to stop playing and John, the river paddler, got away with just a bit of a beating.

I went back around and ran the pour-over again, just in case any of the other ten paddlers who were with us wanted to give it a go. My run was again uneventful due to timing, or was it just luck again? "The more I practise, the luckier I get," is a well-known quote often attributed to the golfer Gary Player. It is known that by attempting the same, or a similar manoeuvre time and again, the result will be an increased chance of success.

Rock hopping is great fun and a good way to build up your ability to read water, kayak-handling skills and confidence. However it is a specialised aspect of sea kayaking with its own risks and hazards. It is most likely to be a group activity and not carried out as a solo experience. There is comfort, and security, in having others around who are able to rescue you and your equipment, should you get it wrong.

EQUIPMENT

A roto-moulded kayak is probably the best option as there will be contact with the rock and pretty much everything else in the vicinity. The shorter the kayak, the easier it will be to manoeuvre when the gaps get smaller. The same goes for paddle choice; a shorter paddle can be moved from side to side more quickly than a longer one and is less likely to become stuck between rocks. A good quality, well-fitting helmet is a must. Neoprene gloves are used by many to give some protection against abrasion by the rock, but at the expense of losing some dexterity with the paddle. If the gloves are thin enough, feel is not reduced to any great extent.

In a slot. Photo: Mark Boyd

SELECTING A ROCK HOP

Spend time observing (see *Reading the Water* chapter). Are the waves going over the rock or through the gulley? Are they coming in sets? What happens when the big waves come through? What happens when the small waves come through? Is there a good place to observe and rescue from?

For a relatively safe rock hop, we are looking for a place that starts in deep water and ends in deep water. That way, even if you get trashed in the middle bit you should end up where you can sort yourself out or be rescued.

THE EDDY BEHIND THE ROCK

This is a good safe place to observe from and to wait and perform rescues if and when they are needed. Any swell will be at a minimum here and most of the water movement will be away from the rock. As long as there is little to be concerned about downwind or downwave, time can be taken to gather people and equipment.

Safe water in the eddy behind a rock.
Photo: Peter Donohue

REHEARSE THE MOVE

By watching how the water is moving around a feature, it is possible to plan how you are going to paddle it. Looking for obvious areas of white turbulent water, areas where the water is flowing and calm spots behind rocks, helps you understand how to achieve a flowing performance as you paddle in and around the rocks. It is better to paddle into a feature having considered how you are going to get out of it, rather than just rushing in. If you are able to plan the moves you need to make, it is then easier to decide what strokes you will use to manoeuvre the kayak through the feature.

GROUP MANAGEMENT AND SAFETY COVER

When rock hopping, there are some particular safety considerations. Often there is a group involved and if there is a free-for-all attitude, things will go wrong. Everyone needs to take an active part in the management of safety and be prepared to carry out a rescue. As there is a lot of moving white water, it is important to be able to read what is happening as the water passes around the feature.

ROLES AND RESPONSIBILITIES

The controller is quite possibly the most important member of the group and is not necessarily the leader. Their job is quite simple; to make sure that there is only one person in the feature at any one time. They hold the power within the group as they will only allow the next paddler through once there is space for a safe passage.

The controller is the person in charge.
Photo: Mark Boyd

The active paddler is the paddler moving through, over or across the feature. They are paddling alone, yet within the safety of a group able to carry out a rescue if needed.

The active paddler. Photo: Roger Aguirre Smith

The safety team is everyone else who is not the controller or the active paddler. It is worth stating, perhaps obviously, that not everyone should be taking photographs when the active paddler is in the feature.

The safety team. Photo: Roger Aguirre Smith

COMMUNICATION

Good communication is needed to allow safe passage through the feature and the means most commonly used are hand signals (see *Paddling in a Group* chapter) rather than voice or whistle. The simple 'thumbs up' works well to let the controller know that the feature is safe for the next paddler to go through. If out of sight, a single long whistle blast works well to signal that all is clear, while three short, sharp blasts indicates that no one is to progress further.

TECHNIQUE

As with all skills development, it is better to start honing your technique on easier and smaller features before moving onto bigger and more complex moves. Never underestimate the power released by the water when it connects with rock and always remember that you are much softer than the rock you are about to hit.

All too often I've been lined up waiting to run some feature or other and, due to my impatience, have gone too early, missing the opportunity of a cushion of water and ending up waiting for the crunch of glass fibre on rock that always follows the mistiming. That said, you definitely have to be bold as you make your moves, hesitating will increase the chances of being in the wrong place as the power of the ocean unleashes itself on the rocks in front of you.

RUNNING A POUR-OVER

Hold your position close to and facing the rock. As the next swell lifts the kayak, time a few strong forward strokes so that the kayak goes over the rock when there is most water between it and the rock. A clean run over and through the pour-over should result.

As the kayak starts on the down slope, perform a low brace on the appropriate side to ensure stability in the aerated, turbulent water. If a turn has to take place, the low brace should be placed on the side towards where the kayak should finish.

Avoid using bow rudder type strokes when travelling quickly past rocks. These vertical strokes put quite a strain on the shoulder joint and contact with a rock, when moving at speed, can often result in injury.

RUNNING A SLOT

The safest option is to go against the flow, as the energy will be pushing you away from the feature and not into it, though it is not possible to go against a significant swell. Whether you choose to go with or against the flow, watch for a while to make sure there are no hidden surprises and then choose your moment.

Paddle with purpose and keep to the best channel within the slot. If the slot is side-on to the swell, it is better to keep close to the rock on the side closest to where the swell is coming from. This gives you a buffer zone, a space you could be swept sideways into, in case a bigger wave than previously observed comes through. Always keep looking to where the waves are coming from, not forgetting any reflected off vertical rocks nearby.

Running a pour-over. Photo: Mark Boyd

Running a slot.

PRACTICE MAKES ...?

Have you ever wondered why some paddlers always manage to be in the right place at the right time, and others are never in this position? It is all to do with experience and practice. With the right type of deliberate practice it is possible to develop your skill more rapidly than by just being on the water.

When developing open skills, varied practice is the best option. By introducing variability into the exercises you are undertaking, you will become more adaptable in your performance. *"Variability leads to adaptability."*

When learning a new skill, or if there is an element of complexity or a chance of injury, take regular breaks during the practice session; this way there will be less chance of becoming fatigued.

GENERAL SAFETY RULES

◎ Generally, if you cannot see the exit, and don't know the section of coast you are paddling, be very cautious.

◎ Familiarity can encourage laziness. If you know the section of coast well, be aware that most incidents happen in areas that are well known to the group.

◎ Keep a good lookout to sea, watching for bigger waves than you are currently playing in. This 'watching for waves' is a whole group activity and if someone sees a much larger wave, then a loud shout of "OUTSIDE" works well to attract attention and signal that there is something big, and normally nasty, coming towards the group.

◎ If you are becoming fatigued, you will make more mistakes.

WARNING

Rock hopping is a very addictive pastime.

It is fun, challenging and will improve your paddling and decision-making skills. If the day is bright and sunny, the white water against the dark blue of the surrounding sea makes it a magical experience; you might also manage to get some great action photos.

Rock hopping at its best. Photo: Roger Aguirre Smith

Surf landing.

Surf Launching and Landing

A group of four of us were paddling in north-west Scotland, from Oldshoremore northwards with the plan of going around Cape Wrath. We were paddling in south-westerly winds of Force 4 to 5 and there was quite a swell running from the west resulting in some fairly lumpy water. As we approached Sandwood Bay we decided to see if landing was possible as this would allow us to have a lunch break ashore.

I went close to the edge of the break first and seeing a rigid inflatable on the beach, decided that this would be a suitable place to land. I checked with the others and paddled towards the shore, backpaddling as the stern of my kayak lifted. I got to shallow water without getting any water over my spraydeck. I signalled for Graeme to come next and being a bit younger, he chose to surf in on the wave that he was on – his wave was about chest high. When he was safe I signalled to Shona to come next. The wave that she was on was at least head high and she was backpaddling when I saw Morag, who was last to come in, bracing into the face of a breaking wave that was somewhere around twice her height, or two metres high. We sorted everything out on shore and got Morag changed into dry clothes.

The owner of the RIB arrived to see if we could help him. He and some friends had been taking pictures of their boats becoming airborne when his came off the top of a wave and overturned, dumping its contents into the water.

We launched after lunch and paddled around the big headland but were unable to stop at our intended place due to the size of the swell. We got some funny looks as we were eating our dinner in the public campsite at 11pm when everyone else was heading to their beds.

Many paddlers do almost everything they can to stay clear of having to launch or land in surf. Surfing in a sea kayak is very different from surfing in a shorter kayak, the forces are much greater and turning takes much longer. When journeying with a heavily-laden kayak, it makes sense to try and avoid surf landings. Look carefully at your charts. It may be that a few miles further on there is a sheltered inlet tucked in the lee of a headland. If a surf landing is inevitable, choose the best place. Perhaps the beach around the corner where the swell will be refracted (see *Reading the Water* chapter) will have smaller and more manageable surf.

If you journey on an exposed coast, you will have to develop the skills to allow you to get on and off the water safely through breaking waves, as sometimes you will have no choice.

SELECTING A SURF BEACH

In the surf zone and its associated white water, it is usually when launching or landing that things can go awry. By paying attention to the conditions, yourself and the group, it is possible to minimise the risks.

Surf offers everything from easy soft play to insane beatings that never seem to stop. When looking for a training venue, try experimenting with different sites; this way you will develop an awareness of how different beaches create different conditions and what to check for when looking at a surf beach. If you don't like the look of it, drive on to the next beach.

THE WAVES

Whether choosing a training venue or a launching or landing place, a major concern is the size of the waves. A one-metre wave, which is about the height of the top of a paddler's head when sitting in their kayak, is manageable with practice, while more than this becomes much more challenging and intimidating.

The frequency that the waves arrive at the beach can also have quite an effect on how it feels. Often the waves come in 'sets' meaning that there will be a period of consistent, similar-sized waves, followed by a period of almost no waves. This 'lull' can be used for launching and landing as long as a good lookout is kept. Watching the horizon for the next approaching set is important and the need to develop the skill cannot be overemphasised.

If the waves are 'stacked', arriving on the beach at very regular intervals and with little time between each wave, the chance of taking a good beating is very high.

RIP CURRENTS

If you can identify a rip (see *Reading the Water* chapter), it can be used to get out to deep water safely. Sometimes this is easy and at other times it can be impossible to see where the rip is.

If you capsize in the rip and you are planning on going out to sea, stay with your kayak and wait until well past the break before attempting an assisted or self rescue.

If you are attempting to get to shore, swim at right angles to the rip, generally parallel to the shore, and keep hold of the seaward end of your kayak. When clear of the rip, swim towards the shore, again keeping your kayak between you and the shore, so that it doesn't get thrown on top of, or into, you.

GROUP MANAGEMENT AND SAFETY COVER

ROLES AND RESPONSIBILITIES

Every group member has a role when landing and launching in surf. Generally speaking, the most experienced paddler should land first and use their height to observe and guide the others in, one at a time. This first person in becomes **the beachmaster;** no one moves without instruction from them, while the last person to land is **the gatekeeper.** Their job is to control who is paddling and manage any safety issues on the water.

The gatekeeper will usually launch first and paddle to beyond where the waves are breaking; they then serve as a target for the other paddlers. **The beachmaster** can help the others into their kayaks and fasten spraydecks before helping with wave selection and timing. As they are last off the beach it goes almost without saying that they should be the most skilled paddler.

COMMUNICATION

Communicating in the surf zone is near impossible if it is not agreed in advance. The means most commonly used are hand signals (see *Paddling in a Group* chapter) rather than voice or whistle.

In addition, there is one specific to surf landing. When someone on shore sees that the paddler has to backpaddle to stop being picked up by a wave, they should signal by holding their paddle horizontally above their head and then lifting and lowering each end alternately.

TECHNIQUE

LAUNCHING

When preparing to launch through surf, take time to just watch the beach. Check where the biggest waves break, where the waves look consistently smaller, and see if you can spot the rip.

Once you have chosen your spot to launch from, bring your kayak close to the water's edge but not so near that it is completely floating. Get in and fit your spraydeck. Holding the paddle in one hand, 'walk' your way to the water by using the paddle blade on the sand in one hand and your other hand on the sand. The main priority is to keep the kayak facing straight into the oncoming waves. If it turns broadside, it becomes very difficult to turn it to face out to sea again.

When you are in water deep enough to paddle, do so. Paddle with purpose and pull hard. When the broken wave reaches you, the kayak will lift up, reach over the top of the wave and pull the kayak over the crest of the foam.

When a wave approaches, you have two choices and these depend on what you can see. If it looks like the wave will not break until you have passed it, paddle hard to clear it (before it does break). Often this is the best option. Keep paddling, as the next wave is likely to be similar and it might be starting to break as you paddle through it.

If the wave does start to break, just keep paddling forward with your body in a forward position, while attempting to reach over the top of the wave to anchor the paddle in the green water beyond. Then keep paddling until you are well clear of the break zone.

If you have timed your launch well you should be able to paddle out through the lull over relatively small waves. On a beach with 'spilling waves', if your timing wasn't quite right, you may be better off paddling slowly forward so as to hold your position in the 'soup' – the broken waves near the beach that have lost most of their power. You are then in a perfect position to paddle hard seaward when the waves further out become less powerful as the next lull arrives.

Timing is critical. Less experienced paddlers often set off from the beach when they see the lull. By the time they get to the critical spot the lull has passed and they take a pasting from the big waves. The trick is to spot the pattern in the sets and start your launch as the

Launching through surf.

last of the big waves come through so that you are on the water and heading out as the lull gets started. One of the most important tasks of the beachmaster is to help less experienced paddlers with their timing.

LANDING

Choose the place to land carefully. Look for any rip currents there might be and areas where the waves appear to be smaller. Paddle towards the beach, keeping a lookout over your shoulder for the next wave. When the rear of your kayak starts to lift, backpaddle strongly enough to stop yourself moving forwards. As soon as the wave has passed below you, paddle forwards with power until the stern starts to lift again. Repeat until you get to the shore. As with launching, timing your run-in is critical.

If you are picked up by a bigger wave, and are thrown towards the beach, lean towards the wave and perform a low brace while moving your bodyweight forwards as much as you can. Keep your elbows as low as possible and keep edging towards the wave. This is to avoid the kayak being tripped up by the dead water on the downwave side. If you do get tripped up, in this position you will be better prepared for a roll as you are almost already completely set up and your shoulders are protected.

Dumping waves are best avoided. If you choose to paddle in on relatively small dumping waves, paddle in slowly until you are as close as possible to where the wave collapses. At this point paddle slowly backwards to hold your position until you see one of the smaller

Landing through surf.

waves approaching. As it goes under you, sprint so as to stay on the back of the wave as it dumps on the shore (you must paddle fast enough to avoid dropping back into the trough and being caught by the next wave), then sprint as high up the beach as the water allows and jump out of your boat quickly to avoid being taken back out by the backwash.

DEVELOPING YOUR SKILLS

After mastering launching and landing, it's time to start playing and having fun in the surf in your sea kayak. The main thing to keep in mind is the size and weight of your boat. When it starts to turn, it will most likely keep on turning until it is broadside to the waves, with little chance of correcting.

With practice it is possible to surf in the green, unbroken section of the wave and change direction by combining carving and skidding turns with plenty of edge, lean and patience. Nothing happens quickly in a long sea kayak when you want it to, but it happens quicker than you expect when you don't. Doing any of this in reverse is probably not the best thing you could do. Not least because you can't see where you are going. If the kayak were to hit the bottom, your back would be in a very vulnerable position and you would most likely injure yourself.

Surfing in control.

AVOIDING A COLLISION

The best way to avoid a collision is to stay well away from other kayakers. Sooner or later though it will happen. You will be having the best run of the day and there will be someone right in your path. If you are on the wave, shout loudly to attract the attention of the person you are heading towards, try to slow your kayak as much as possible and turn it away from the impact.

If a collision seems likely, the best thing to reduce the chance of damage and injury is for **both** paddlers to capsize and remain in their kayak for as long as they feel able. Both kayaks will have slowed and if a collision does take place, it is likely to be much reduced. If the paddlers are able to, rolling upright is the best scenario, but if this fails then a wet exit and swim to shore is a reasonable option.

Avoiding a collision.

Kylerhea tide race.

Paddling in a Tide Race

It was the group's first time in a tide race of more than three knots. All six had previous experience of overfalls and surfing in sea kayaks and they could all rescue and self rescue. The briefing on the slip, as we prepared to launch, was thorough, and I remember saying, "If you end up in the water and there is no one close to you, start swimming with your kayak and paddle towards the Glenelg shoreline; it'll only take half an hour".

We were in Kylerhea, on the south-going flow, it was close to springs and the wind was from the south. As we launched we could see the first waves of the race and as we approached, we turned to face upstream. The plan was to catch these lovely green waves, surf them for a bit and paddle back towards the Skye shore to regroup.

When we started surfing, one of the group capsized and their buddy started the rescue while I kept an overview of the whole group. By the time the rescue was complete, we had drifted south into the bigger mess of standing waves where another capsize occurred. This time, there was no buddy to perform the rescue as everyone was focused on their own safety and had little awareness of anyone else on the water.

I went in to perform the rescue, and as I was finishing, the first person capsized again and I had to contact tow them. Initially, I tried to make my way towards where the other paddler in the water was, but he was swimming as instructed towards Glenelg. Once my casualty was in the eddy where they were happy, I told them to head for the corner of the beach which the others were aiming for.

Confident that the rest of the group were now safe, I paddled back towards the swimmer and offered a rescue, but it was declined as he wanted to test my theory that if you were in the water, you would end up on the beach in thirty minutes.

I stayed close just in case he became tired and needed a rescue, and could see all the others approach and then land on the beach. Within thirty minutes we had indeed landed where I had said, and although the swimmer was tired, he was elated that he had been able to swim positively for the time it had taken to get out of the race to a safe landing.

SELECTING A TIDE RACE

The main thing I look for when paddling in a tide race is a safe run-out. Where is the water calm enough to perform rescues? Where are there eddies, beaches or inlets where we could arrange to regroup?

There are typically two different types of tide race; where the flow is off a headland, and where the flow is between two pieces of land. They behave differently and require different safety considerations.

OFF A HEADLAND

With the first type, the direction of the flow is generally offshore. If there is an incident, everything gets carried away from land and any rescues have to take place offshore. If there is wind or swell opposing the water flow, the conditions may remain rough for quite some distance. By knowing where there is an eddy, you can make your way to easier water.

IN A SOUND OR CHANNEL

The second type takes place between two pieces of land and the flow is generally in line with the land on either side. Normally, there are eddies on both sides of the main flow which starts to dissipate as soon as the narrowing stops. When an incident occurs in the main part of the flow, things start to calm down relatively quickly. If there is land on both sides, gathering everything together should be straightforward.

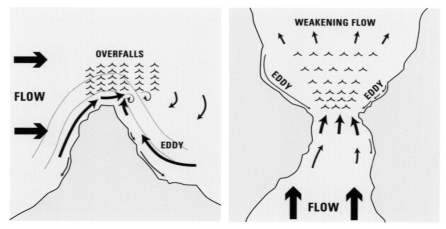

Headland tide race.   *Channel tide race.*

GROUP MANAGEMENT AND SAFETY COVER

Tidal flows are quite possibly the most challenging environments a sea kayaker will face when managing a group. Everything is moving in relation to everything else, it is generally noisy enough so that voice commands are difficult to hear, and if a paddler ends up in the water, separated from their kayak, they will be going in different directions. The best position for a leader is to be downstream of the rest of the group, so that if something does happen, they should be in the best place to deal with it.

ROLES AND RESPONSIBILITIES

Everyone has a safety role and must be constantly looking out for all the other group members. Staying in control of your kayak is as fundamental as staying upright; if it is out of control, it will take you where the flow directs it. By knowing when to back off and return to the eddy, many incidents can be avoided.

COMMUNICATION

VHF radios can work if the paddlers can take their hands off the paddle shaft long enough to be able to work the controls. This does lead to instability in many cases though, and most people will end up simply listening to the broadcast perhaps unable to do anything to help someone close to them. If close enough to one another, simple hand signals work well, but voice works best of all as understanding can be checked.

GENERAL SAFETY RULES

Surfing waves in a tide race is very similar to surfing waves on a beach, with the added bonus of not having shallow water to deal with. The bigger difference is that the waves are less predictable and could come from many directions at the same time.

Here is a list of simple ways to keep out of trouble:

◎ If you are heading towards someone, try to slow down, change your course and shout to them that you are likely to collide. If a collision seems inevitable, both you and they should be prepared to capsize and roll, and after a pause, self rescue or be rescued.

◎ It is very easy and quick to become separated in a tide race, so care must be taken to ensure this does not happen. Paddling in a buddy system with both halves of the pair looking out for each other is a good option.

◎ If the race is small it may be that the leader sits in the eddy and has everyone come to them after a period of play. If something goes wrong, they are in a good position to offer assistance while ensuring the safety of the others.

◎ Always agree a rendezvous place and time so that everyone can come together.

JOURNEYING

If the plan is to safely paddle a stretch of coastline, then you may choose to avoid a tide race by planning to arrive at slack water.

If you arrive at anything other than slack, then you have three options. One is to go further out to sea, the second is to stay closer inshore to avoid the most turbulent area. If you choose the third and decide to run through the race, keep as close together as possible without getting in each other's way. If a group member capsizes, a good option is to wait until you have flushed into the calm water after the tide race before carrying out a rescue.

PLAYING

When choosing to go into a tide race to train or play, the first consideration is to select the best time. Just after maximum flow is good as the flow will be decreasing rather than increasing, meaning that conditions will start to lessen. An alternative is to get there just after slack and build up confidence and skills while the race steadily increases in power. It is important that you are able to recognise when it is time to stop.

I always like to check that there is a run-out or safe place downstream where it is possible to recover any stray pieces of equipment. If someone does capsize, then a quick rescue is an option, as long as everyone is confident in performing one. The casualty has to ensure that they are visible, and the best way to achieve this is to hold their paddle vertical and keep facing the other group members as much as possible. Often the water can be so turbulent as to fill the kayak with water as soon as the casualty is back in the cockpit, in this case a contact or rafted tow will work until a calmer area is reached.

In a tide race.

Setting off into the night.

Paddling at Night

I am of the sea, yet I am of the land also. I have a story to tell, one of observation and awareness. It was a dark night, the new moon was just showing its silver crescent, and the currents were flowing swiftly as is always the case at this time of the month. The water was flat and there was no wind to speak of, which added to the atmosphere.

Overhead, the northern lights or aurora borealis were dancing their way across the night sky, shimmering green and yellow, often rising to a red azimuth. I knew that there was a lot of biolumi-nescence after the inlet, just to the east of where you were launching, as I had just come that way.

I watched you dress and carry your kayaks to the water's edge. I watched you all check that you had a glowing light attached to you and that you had a much brighter light that pierced the blackness, and looked like a giant's eye when it was switched on.

These bright lights were extinguished as you got onto the water and then you started count-ing – "*One, two, three* ..." all the way to "*six*". Communication is so much easier when you are able to do so using simple words.

You set off cautiously along the inlet, perhaps knowing that there were shallow areas, perhaps thinking that there were obstructions, but not really knowing, as your sight had been reduced to the area around each of you, with its glowing light.

I stayed out of sight behind you all, following at a distance I felt comfortable with. I could hear everything you were saying and feel the anxiety rising well before you lit up the night with your bright lights. As you went into the shallows, I chose not to follow, instead going the other way around the small islet and waiting for you on the other side.

Your lights were off now and it was here that the bioluminescence was at its peak. I watched the whirlpool-like vortices that swirled off your paddles as you made progress, I watched the outline your kayaks made as they cut through the water and I watched as fish darted all over the place. I made you watch, and gasp, as I swam below your kayaks, rolling to face you as I passed so that I could see the look on your faces.

The dark blue of the deep water with its streaks of bioluminescence seemed to be mirrored in the black of the night sky. The aurora and the Milky Way reflecting on the water only added to the impression of flying.

As you set off, heading east, I skirted around the back of you all making sure that you stayed together and no one was left behind. When one of you got a bit separated from the others, I cleared my throat and immediately heard counting start with *"Five, Six, One, two ..."*. I followed you all of that night, only making my presence known when one of you was not as close as you should have been to the rest of the group. When you went safely ashore, I stayed in the water, for I am not of the land completely.

EVERYTHING CHANGES WHEN IT IS DARK – MONSTERS EVERYWHERE

Conditions benignly paddled in during the day, become unrecognisable at night. Waves appear bigger, the wind feels stronger and the temperature really does drop.

Monsters are everywhere. The psychological difference is that one of our senses – sight, has been muted to such an extent that we have to use others to replace it. Our hearing becomes enhanced, every sound is amplified making it difficult to judge how far away a noise actually is. If you happen to pass close to a heronry, you will hear screeches that will make the hairs stand up on the back of your neck. If it is calm, sound seems to travel much further over water in the dark compared with during the day. It is often possible to hear engines starting and people on land coughing while still a long way away.

Other senses are heightened too – you will be much more aware of how the kayak feels and how it is moving through the water. You might even be able to smell the local restaurant preparing dinner.

PREPARATION

Night paddling doesn't just feel different, there are also physical changes that need to be taken into account. By preparing for night paddling, there is more chance that everything will fall into place when it is needed rather than ending up in some unplanned adventure.

LIGHTING

Some form of personal lighting is essential. Make sure lights have fresh batteries, or at least that a fresh set is easily available.

APPROPRIATE CLOTHING

It is important that everyone takes charge of their own comfort by ensuring they have adequate clothing to cope with whatever the climate may throw at them. For example, in the Scottish Highlands, hail showers can occur at any time of the year and the temperature can drop by 5°C.

No matter how warm you are during the day, you will feel colder at night. If possible, go ashore before it gets dark, have a snack and a warm drink, put on another layer on top and a warm hat. Make sure your storm cag is easily accessible and take spare warm hats, perhaps in a dry bag in the day hatch, in case yours gets wet or someone loses theirs.

WHEN ASHORE

This is always a good time to check on your location and arrange the lights so that they work efficiently for identification and illumination. If you are walking around, avoid dazzling your companions. If your headtorch is lit, have it around your neck rather than on your head, this way the light shines downwards and not into the eyes of the person you are talking to.

Headtorch around neck.

LIGHTING AND VISIBILITY

Night paddlers need different lights for different purposes.

You need to show an all-round white light so that other water users know of your presence, this doubles as a marker light so that the others in your group can locate you. This can be a low intensity light and there are a few options on the market.

A high intensity light (usually in the form of a powerful headtorch) is great for finding a piece of lost equipment, or illuminating someone in the water. This same high intensity light is also invaluable when approaching the shoreline and coming ashore. When ashore there is normally not the same need for a high intensity light, and something a bit more modest will serve for general illumination.

Different light sources.

A low intensity light is necessary to read a chart (see *Retaining night vision* section below).

PERSONAL MARKER LIGHT

A low intensity marker light should be as high up on the paddler as possible – the top of the head is the best place, as it allows all-round visibility. If placed on the rear of the buoyancy aid where it is completely out of the paddler's sight, it can be obscured by their body when viewed from anywhere other than directly behind. Attaching it into or onto the headtorch band is as good as anything else I've tried. A simple glow stick or snaplight works well but they tend to go out of date, which reduces the brightness and sometimes the glow is so slight that it is of no use. An electronic glow light is good as it is less harmful to the environment and lasts longer than the disposable type.

Low intensity lights.

RETAINING NIGHT VISION

There has been much research into what colour of light is best for maintaining night vision. Traditionally, red was the favoured choice but more recently green has risen in popularity.

The intensity of the light is more important than the colour. Green, however, allows us to see information that is hidden when using a red light. When using a chart at night much of the information disappears under a red light, while the green one allows better differentiation between the printed colours.

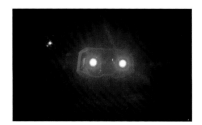

Red light.

Use a light, of whatever colour works for you, that is sufficiently bright to allow you to carry out the task at hand. Everyone is different and what we see differs greatly, especially in low light conditions. It is important to test what works best for you. I use a normal headtorch with a sliding diffuser, which I have coloured with a spirit

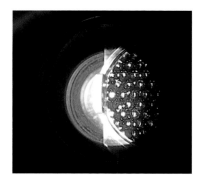

Modified headtorch.

marker pen. This transmits enough white light to let me see a chart properly without any distortion of colour but doesn't affect my night vision. If I need more light, I simply slide the diffuser to the side.

RETRO-REFLECTIVE MARKING

Unless your goal is to remain hidden from view, everything should have retro-reflective patches applied, to allow identification in low light. Available as sew-on material and self-adhesive sheets, it is an inexpensive way to mark your position. In testing carried out by the British Royal Air Force, it was found that a single 25mm x 25mm square of retro-reflective material on top of a helmet resulted in a 400% increase in likelihood of being found at night on the sea.

Many pieces of paddling equipment now come with reflective strips and patches but there are some which do not. Paddles are expensive pieces of equipment, and the most expensive ones are made from carbon fibre, which is black. On the water at night, these almost disappear, and if dropped into the water they become invisible. By putting strips of reflective tape on both sides of the blade and perhaps around the joins between the blades and the shaft, you will transform your paddle into a glowing stick when a light is shone on it.

Applying the same reflective tape to the kayak assists in identification and if some thought is put into it, the results will be visible from all directions. Even a 1cm^2 piece of retro-reflective tape will be seen from a considerable distance. Over time the material will degrade resulting in a drop in performance, so monitor the reflective properties of the patches and replace them before they fail completely.

Retro-reflective tape.

Be aware that although some manufacturers put retro-reflective patches onto the sleeves of paddling jackets, they are often in the wrong place if you are trying to attract attention. When facing a prospective rescuer and waving at them, the underside of the arm is towards them, but the retro-reflective patch is generally on the top of the arm and can only be seen from behind.

GROUP CONTROL

Generally, at night, it is important to keep group control tighter than during the day. With reduced senses, especially sight, most people like to be closer to others when they can't see them well. Communication is easier too with everyone closer together.

A realistic way to keep track of everyone while on the water at night is for the members of the group to number themselves. Starting with "one" and going to as many as are in the group, this way everyone has a unique number identifier. Normally the leader starts the count and the others take their turn – "*One – two – three – four – five – six*" – if there are six group members. At any time if anyone feels that they do not know where they are in relation to the others, they can start the count from their number, the other group members should continue the count until the originator is reached.

This works well as long as everyone remembers their number and shouts it out at the appropriate time. It is not unusual for someone to remind number *four* that they have to shout out their number. Within a small group of paddlers who know each other, it can be simpler to shout out your name as this will feel much less formal than the numbering method.

POSITION RELATIVE TO LIGHT SOURCE

Every time you paddle at night, experiment with the best position relative to a light source that allows you to see the other paddlers. By positioning yourself between a source of light, such as the moon, lights on the shore, etc. and the paddlers, the light will illuminate everything thus allowing you to see clearly. The kayaks will appear in their normal colours, with anything white showing up particularly well.

Position relative to light source.

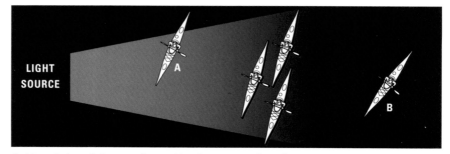

Position relative to light source: from position A you can see colours, from position B you can see silhouettes.

On the other hand, by being on the dark side, the other paddlers in the group will show up as silhouettes against the lighter background. Even on the darkest of nights, there is enough residual glow in the sky to allow these outlines to appear. Identification will be reduced to counting the number of paddlers, rather than a positive identification of each individual. This is when a low intensity marker light works spectacularly well if it is positioned thoughtfully.

Silhouette.

RESCUES AT NIGHT

Rescues in the dark become much more intense as there is a much greater chance of something becoming misplaced or lost. Everyone should stay very close together and all should have headtorches on and illuminating the paddler(s) in the water. The major downside to this though is the resulting loss of night vision – when the lights are extinguished it becomes very dark.

Rescue in the dark.

Towing.

Towing

Paddling from Village Bay to Glen Bay on Hirta, the outermost island group in Britain, I realised after about ten minutes that I did not have my tow system with me. It was tied onto the guardrails of our mothership the MV Cuma. I told Murty, the group leader, and we agreed that it would not be a problem as he had a spare waist tow in his day hatch, and if we needed it we could access it easily while on the water.

We had a lovely morning exploring the south-east coast of the island, going into the caves that were not too affected by the swell coming in from the Atlantic. The wind was blowing about 12 knots and gusting 20 or so but, as we were in the lee, we were protected from it.

As we approached Glen Bay we came to an arch which is considered the normal route around the corner. Unfortunately the swell was a bit big to go through, so as a group, we went around the end of the rock. This was when the wind hit us. Three people capsized on the first gust and nine were left upright.

Ken was out in front with four paddlers who had not been blown over and they made their way to the Cuma, which was less than 400 metres from us. Murty had one of the casualties to deal with, while I had the other two; we both had an assistant. We performed the rescues and I realised that we were some 100 metres apart. I took Morag's deck tow and got her to tie it onto my deck line behind the cockpit with as many knots as she could fit into the tail of line, as the last thing I wanted was for it to come off and have to go through the procedure a second time. I then towed a raft of three to the Cuma, this took around 45 minutes due to the strength of the wind. When we arrived at the tender, Ken and the others were waiting to help everyone aboard.

With the three people I had been towing safe, I turned around and went back to help Murty who had two in tow and had been a bit further out to sea when we had been hit by the wind. I clipped onto the front of his kayak and we did an in-line tow, getting to the tender as the last of the previous group were climbing onto the Cuma.

Whenever you undertake a journey, there is a possibility that you will need to tow another kayaker. Almost every time you have to deal with an emergency situation, towing is involved in some shape or form. As you will have realised from reading the above, it pays to make sure you have your tow system with you.

CONTACT TOWS

As the name suggests, contact tows involve contact between the rescuer and the casualty. There are many ways to perform a contact tow, some involve pieces of equipment specifically designed for the purpose, others use makeshift gear, while others still use nothing more than the rescuer and the casualty.

A contact tow is most often used when there is a chance that any given situation could quickly get out of hand. Examples are:

◎ When the casualty has dropped or broken their paddle while close to rocks and is being pushed onto them.

◎ To stabilise a situation in order to buy time. This allows thinking time to decide on what type of tow to set up.

◎ When anxiety or fear has taken over and the casualty requires a bit more support in order to take them to a safer place.

END TOGGLE

The most straightforward contact tow is for the casualty to hold onto the rescuer's kayak. The rescuer approaches the casualty from 90° and allows them to hold onto the end toggle. The rescuer then paddles away gently while the casualty continues to hold on. This works well if there is wind blowing both parties onto rocks or other obstacles. The downside is that there is much resistance, as the casualty's kayak is being pulled sideways.

Holding contact tow. Photo: Angus Mackie

END OF THE KAYAK

Another approach is for the rescuer to come alongside and to have the casualty hold onto their kayak, either at the front or at the rear. The casualty can lean onto the rescuer's kayak to gain support. However, paddling efficiency and manoeuvrability are reduced.

Leaning contact tow. Photo: Angus Mackie

DECK LINE

Possibly the most efficient is to have the casualty facing the rescuer and sitting upright. The casualty holds the deck line of the rescuer's kayak with the hand closest to the rescuer and pulls towards them. They use the other hand to hold the end of the kayak and push it away from them.

Holding the deck line and the end of the boat.
Photo: Angus Mackie

This forms a stable triangular support and ensures that the kayaks stay together making the rescuer's task easier. If turning becomes an issue, the casualty moves towards the rescuer and holds on in the same manner closer to the centre of the kayak. This effectively shortens the overall length and allows easier manoeuvring.

Move to the centre of the kayak to increase manoeuvrability. Photo: Angus Mackie

SHOCK CORD TOGGLE TOW

This involves a little bit of preparation at home. Cut two pieces of deck elastic around 30cm long and, using a simple overhand knot, tie them to make two loops. Tape the ends to stop them fraying. Before launching, attach each loop using a lark's foot hitch around your deck lines, close to the cockpit, one on each side. The overhand knot must face upwards. This is so that when the toggle of the casualty's kayak is inserted through the loop, it will become trapped between the parallel elastics.

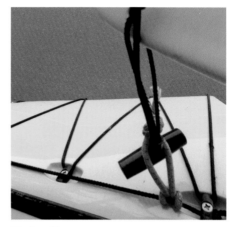

Shock cord loops.

To start the tow, if the casualty's kayak has a clip holding the toggle to stop it moving, unclip this to allow the toggle to hang down. The toggle is then pushed through one of the shock cord loops mounted earlier and towing can begin.

To release, all that is required is to turn the toggle so that it disengages from the elastic. These loops work particularly well on an empty kayak when there is less weight to be moved.

CLASSIC CONTACT TOW

A strong cord, a kayak's width in length (about 60cm), around 6mm in diameter with an easily deployed clip on each end, has been the classic piece of equipment for contact towing for many years. Either end can be clipped to the casualty's kayak.

For a short towline, attach one clip to your kayak, pass the cord through the deck lines of the casualty's kayak and double it back, making the second clip fast to your kayak.

Classic contact tow.

For a longer towline, attach one clip to the casualty's kayak and the other to yours. The longer the line, the more movement there will be, with the risk that the casualty's kayak connects with the rescuer's chest when it is least expected.

MODIFIED CLASSIC CONTACT TOW

For the modified classic, a cord approximately three times the width of a kayak (1.8m) is used, with clips on both ends. The ends are passed below the deck lines on both sides, then crossed over to the opposite side of the kayak and secured, ready for deployment. Alternatively, the ends can be crossed again and attached back to their own side.

The longer line gives a greater choice of length of towline when being deployed; short, long or very long. It could also be used to make a bridle when setting up a distance tow (see the section on *Distance tows* below).

Modified classic contact tow. Photo: Angus Mackie

Modified classic contact tow.

BODY-MOUNTED CONTACT TOW

In addition to their main towing system, many people carry a towline that attaches around their waist or to a chest harness, developed for white water rescue.

With practice, this works well but there are some associated issues:

- ◎ A kayak attached to your body at close range can be an intimidating experience in anything other than flat water.

- ◎ The attachment point on a chest harness is generally too high on the body to allow for efficient paddling.

- ◎ The extra leverage placed on the upper body is extreme.

APPROACH

When positioning yourself to perform a contact tow, it is almost always better to manoeuvre into the space between the hazard and the casualty. Generally, the wind will be blowing both the rescuer and the casualty towards the hazard and turning will be difficult. By paddling into this space, you will start to move the casualty away from the obstacle, simply by your momentum, as you make contact with the casualty's kayak. The image below shows how the rescuer's kayak is able to turn as the bow and stern are both free.

If the casualty is closest to the rock, with the rescuer on the outside, it will be more difficult for the rescuer to turn into the wind because their kayak will not be free at either end.

Contact tow away from rock with rescuer between rock and casualty. Photo: Angus Mackie

IMPORTANT POINTS TO CONSIDER WHEN CONTACT TOWING

◎ Use elastic only for the toggle tow, not for any of the other methods as it has too much give, and if it detaches, the clip becomes a missile.

◎ As the towline is always within reach, it does not require a quick-release method. A body-mounted type does. That said, you should always carry a knife or line cutter in case of entanglement.

◎ A contact tow is generally used only over short distances to stabilise a situation and allow time to set up a more efficient distance tow.

◎ Practise contact towing often, so that when you come to use it for real, it will be second nature.

TYPE OF CLIP

The type of clip used in any towing scenario has to meet a few simple rules:

◎ The gate must not be able to snag. Most climbing karabiners have a notch that exactly matches the diameter of most kayak deck lines. This can make attaching and releasing the clip from the casualty's kayak difficult.

◎ It must be simple to use, even with cold hands or when wearing gloves.

◎ It must be strong enough to take the weight and shock load of three kayaks and three rescuers towing. I don't recommend the use of plastic clips. They always seem to release by straightening and returning to their original shape, especially in warm weather.

◎ It should be small enough so as not to accidentally self clip between two kayaks.

Different types of clip.

133

DISTANCE TOWS

Carrying a towing system and knowing how to use it correctly without injuring yourself or anyone else is a key skill of safe sea kayaking. Always have a knife or line cutter close to hand when using rope in water as you never know when you may have to cut yourself, or someone else, free.

There are two main types of distance tow systems, and they both have similar features.

BODY TOW

The waist-mounted towline is the most versatile, as it can be used with any kayak and can be passed to another group member.

It includes a belt with a quick-release buckle that should always be accessible and not hidden under the buoyancy aid. The tail of the waist belt should protrude through the buckle by the minimum amount to give a secure grip. If the tail is too long, the webbing can fold and may become trapped in the quick-release buckle.

Body tow.

When you measure up for your towline and are trimming the end of the webbing, make sure that you are wearing your winter kayaking layers and equipment. It would not be the first time that a belt has been shortened in the summer, only for its owner to find that it is too short for winter use.

With waist-mounted tow systems, all of the strain is passed through a narrow part of the body. One real benefit though, is that the rescuer can feel every slight change in tension, such as if the casualty capsizes or becomes snagged on something. For people with a short back, a boat-mounted system may be a better option as the strain is mostly taken through the fittings on the kayak.

The minimum amount of tail. Photo: Angus Mackie

BOAT TOW

The boat-mounted version requires specialist fittings on the kayak in order to use it safely. This means that its use is limited to kayaks with these fittings.

There needs to be a 'bullseye' or fairlead situated on the centre line of the kayak, behind the cockpit. If you look at how a tug tows a bigger ship, the towing attachment is very close behind the wheelhouse so that the tug can manoeuvre. This should be reinforced on the inside of the kayak with large washers or a plate to spread the load. There is also a need for a cam cleat, which traps the line but allows it to release when required. The cam cleat will require some maintenance every now and again. Washing it with fresh water and applying some type of lubricant will keep it working as it should. There also needs to be a place to secure the towline storage bag.

Boat tow. Photo: Angus Mackie

Cam cleat and bullseye.

TOWLINE DESIGN

Over years of towing, I have found a towline design that can cover almost every eventuality and minimises the risks to both the rescuer and casualty. It works waist-mounted or deck-mounted, with a few variations.

The overall length of the tow should be between ten and fifteen metres. Floating line of 6mm in diameter is good as it is

A towline for every eventuality.

strong enough and easy to handle with cold, wet hands. It should be brightly coloured to make it more visible.

I will describe the towline, starting at the end that is attached to the casualty's kayak.

ATTACHMENT CLIP

All of the points I made above about clips apply here too. The possibility of snagging is something that needs to be at the forefront of your consciousness at all times. To attach the clip to the line, my preference is to stitch through the line and then whip, or tape, the end to provide a good secure fitting with a low profile. Knots of any type always seem to snag on the deck lines of the towed kayak.

CLEAN LINE

Next, there needs to be a length of 'clean' line without knots or floats. This should measure approximately half the length of a kayak (2.5 metres) to reduce the risk of snagging.

FLOAT

Immediately after the clean line, there needs to be a float, ideally a bullet or torpedo type, not the donut type as this will most likely snag and never release.

SHOCK ABSORBER

The most suitable place for a shock absorber in the system is immediately after the float, as this does not interfere with the operation and keeps it out of the way of the chain coil and release system. When a shock absorber is used, it should be incorporated in such a manner that if it breaks, the integrity of the rest of the system is not compromised.

CHAIN COIL

From the shock absorber, the line is chain coiled until the shortening clip is reached (see opposite).

SHORTENING CLIP

The shortening clip is tied into the line close to the rescuer's end. It is important that it is fixed and not able to travel down the line, out of reach. Clip the last loop of the chain coil into it, to stop it unravelling. This keeps the towline short and easy to manage.

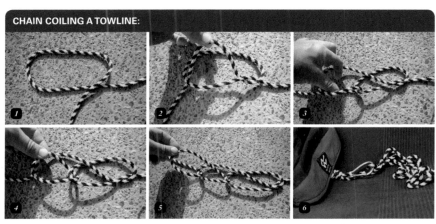

CHAIN COILING A TOWLINE:

Chain coiling a towline.

RESCUER'S END

This is where the waist-mounted version differs slightly from the deck-mounted.

The attachment to the waist belt needs a bit of thought and often the line is tied into a clip or loop of tape within the bag. The most positive method of attachment is to tie the line directly around the belt webbing, leaving a bit of slack to attach another line to extend the system if a greater distance between rescuer and casualty is required.

For the deck-mounted system, a length of clean line is needed after the knot that fixes the shortening clip. This is so that the clip is beyond the stern of the kayak and the clean line is running over the rear deck, reducing the chance of snagging.

This line feeds through the bullseye and cam cleat and allows for a clean release. Re-attaching it is easy by passing the tail through the bullseye then through the cam cleat.

STORAGE BAG

The storage bag must allow the line and float to deploy, and make it easy to re-stow the system after use. A split plastic D ring attached to the bag provides a secure anchor point for the clip until it is needed. It

Plastic split D ring.

won't be necessary to unclip from this D ring as a sharp tug will release the clip from the bag, saving time when it is critical.

It is useful to have another split D ring fitted on the buoyancy aid, in a place where it feels natural to have the towline clipped. If you are expecting to have to tow, this saves a considerable amount of time. It also gives a good reattachment point when the tow is completed and you are tidying the line but not re-stowing it into the bag.

Waist towline in front. Photo: Angus Mackie

BODY TOWLINE IN FRONT

The waist towline is easier to use if you have it resting in front (on your belly). This way it is possible to approach the casualty from either side and, using the hand on the same side as the casualty's kayak, clip directly. The bag is then moved round to the back. There is less chance of the line snagging on the buoyancy aid than when it is passed over the head from the back.

WHERE AND HOW TO CLIP

When clipping onto a casualty's kayak it is important to do so in a way that does not strain the kayak fittings more than necessary.

ONE KAYAK

A single clip onto a single deck line near the front of the kayak is best, as this spreads the load between all of the deck fittings. In the case of the front fitting breaking, the tow will stay attached. Clipping to the line closest to the rescuer's kayak, and always from below, ensures a lower chance of it detaching.

Clipping the deck line. Photo: Angus Mackie

Do not pass the towline beneath one deck line and attach it back onto the rescuer's bag to shorten it. I have seen a few deck lines severed when the towline pulls through the casualty's deck line, due to heat build up (or 'weld-abrade'). To overcome this, one option is to clip a karabiner onto the deck line of the casualty's kayak, then pass the rescuer's towline through this. It allows a smooth and free-running action by reducing the friction.

Another good option is to use a bridle. Using the modified classic contact towline, double the line and tie an overhand knot in the centre. The clips are then attached onto the deck lines behind a deck fitting on the bow and the loop is left to dangle below the kayak.

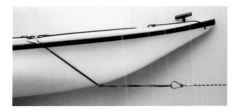

The tow is connected to the loop. Often a towed kayak becomes unstable, especially if the sea is choppy, because the towline twists the kayak. A bridle is more stable and helps the bow rise up out of the waves.

Bridle.

MULTIPLE KAYAKS

Sometimes a tow involves an assistant who is supporting the casualty. In this case the rescuer will be towing both the casualty and the assistant. Several options work but the assistant always needs to be able to let go, if the situation dictates.

Pass the towline through the assistant's deck line before clipping onto the casualty's kayak. This way the assistant can move forwards and re-lease the tow clip from the casualty. The towline will pull out from the deck lines of both kayaks. If it should become snagged in the assistant's deck line, the assistant and casualty must keep hold of one another and the casualty can move forwards and release the tow from the assistant's kayak.

Assistant and casualty. Photo: Angus Mackie

Casualty holding on while moving forward to release a snagged line. Photos: Joe Hughes

When clipped in this manner the two towed kayaks form a V. Photo: Angus Mackie

With this method of attachment, the towed kayaks form a V shape in the direction of travel. This increases the drag for the rescuer but does give a more stable platform for the assistant and casualty.

To reduce the chances of snagging, a 'dog-lead' can be used; this is a length of cord or tape (2.5m) with a clip on the end.

A 'dog-lead'.

The clip is attached to the casualty's kayak behind the second deck fitting, near the front hatch, and passed through the assistant's deck line in the same place. The end of the 'dog-lead' is passed to the assistant who can tie it off to their kayak using a highwayman's hitch, other release knot, or just hold onto it. There is not a lot of pull on this end so holding onto it is an option if nothing else needs doing to help the casualty. The rescuer clips their towline onto the 'dog-lead' between the two kayaks. With this method, both the rescuer and the assistant can release from the tow. If the assistant releases, then everyone is completely free of the system.

Releasing from the 'dog-lead' tow.
Photo: Angus Mackie

DISTANCE TOWING ISSUES

There are a number of distance towing factors that you need to be aware of.

KEEP IT AS SHORT AS POSSIBLE

Towing is an emergency technique used to either remove someone from immediate danger or help a very tired paddler. The leader needs to come up with a plan that keeps the towing distance as short as possible. Perhaps you only need to tow them clear of the danger or to calmer water. Perhaps you need to get them to the nearest landing place where you can sort things out and rest before continuing the journey. You may even need to consider shortening the trip.

SPEED VERSUS THOROUGHNESS

The less urgent a tow is, the more time can be taken to set it up properly and make it easier for the rescuer. When there is a lot going on, whether that is proximity to rocks in breaking water, the risk of being swept away in a tidal flow or any other time-pressured situation, the best thing to do is connect a tow and start paddling to a safer area.

CONTROLLING THE LINE

It is important to control the line to stop it snagging on the rear end of the rescuer's kayak. Should this happen, it would make it very difficult for the rescuer to turn their kayak.

Awareness is all that is needed, and to move the line to the other side of the stern. If the casualty's kayak is off to the left, the rescuer reaches around with their left hand and flicks the line to the left side. This is something that needs to be practised often in order that the correct hand is used and not just the preferred one. If the casualty is off to the right, then the rescuer has to flick the line over their kayak with their right hand.

Line caught around the stern followed by reach and flick. Photos: Joe Hughes

If anything is carried on the rear deck then snagging becomes a real hazard. Spare paddles, a stirrup pump or a bag of essential equipment all create an almost perfect trap for a released towline. They also catch on the towline as it is in operation and can make it almost impossible for the rescuer to release without a third party.

It would be ironic if a flare container was the reason the emergency services had to be called out to perform a rescue.

Paddle trap.
Photo: Angus Mackie

Pump trap.
Photo: Angus Mackie

TIDAL STREAMS

When towing in even the most gentle of tidal streams, great care has to be taken when man-oeuvring near obstacles. When crossing upstream of a hazard, there is a real possibility of drifting onto it, and the towline becoming caught around it. The hazard could be a bridge pillar, a moored boat in an estuary or a buoy. It is best to avoid towing near such hazards unless it is absolutely essential.

RELEASING THE TOW

When releasing the tow, take care to ensure the whole system is moved away from your body before letting it drop. Hold onto the release until you have checked everything is clear.

Releasing the tow from a body tow (left) and from a boat tow (right).
Photo: Angus Mackie

CHECKING YOU CAN RELEASE THE TOW

An extremely useful exercise is to capsize while towing. Release the tow underwater, then either roll upright, or wet exit and carry out a self rescue, before collecting the tow and re-stowing it.

This should be practised with other paddlers to provide safety, as there is a chance that the line will become entangled and hinder the exit or roll.

If the casualty reverse-paddles gently, the line will come free more easily.

Underwater release. Photo: Jake McInnes

MULTIPLE RESCUER TOWS

Having more than one rescuer involved in towing makes it faster and less strenuous. In the rare case where a person needs to be towed for a long distance, this is the best way to go about it. There are two main methods.

IN-LINE TOW

The in-line tow works by adding one or more people towing in front of the main rescuer. The power transmitted to the towed kayaks is increased significantly. This is used when there is a need to move the whole assembly more quickly. The person towing closest to the casualty's kayak takes most of the strain as they have the raft holding them back and the power of the people in front pulling them forward.

In-line tow. Photo: Angus Mackie

Good communication is the key to making this work well and it is imperative that one person, the spotter, stays free of the system and maintains contact between the front and the back of the tow. There is the possibility that one of the people in the middle of the tow could be pulled sideways and this has to be sorted as soon as it happens. The spotter has to be more like an orchestrator than a commander, but not afraid to command when required.

Due to the distance from the front to the back of the tow, the spotter needs to ensure the person in the lead doesn't cut corners. If each person cuts a bit more, the people being towed end up on the wrong side of the very hazard that is being avoided.

Everyone must have a knife or rope cutter easily available as there is a vast amount of line about.

V TOW

A V tow works with two people towing. Both are clipped directly onto the casualty and paddle next to each other at the same speed. Unless well practised, this method does not work well.

If one rescuer pulls more strongly than the other, the result is that the other rescuer gets pulled out of line. Their towline will lie in a loop in the water and start to create drag. There is also a risk that the slower rescuer will be pulled in reverse. This has to be avoided, as the time required to rectify the situation could lead to the group drifting towards the very hazard they are trying to avoid.

DRAG

The amount of drag acting on a towline when it is lying in a loop between two kayaks is incredible.

Let's assume that the line is 15m metres long and 8mm in diameter; the resultant drag is the equivalent of a drogue 35cm x 35cm, and this is before you add things like a shock absorber or a float into the equation. Equally, if the bag in which the towline is stored ends up in the water, the drag effect is substantial.

When towing, it is important that the spotter, or whoever is out in front, keeps a good lookout for the line starting to drag. If it does, the front paddler will have to paddle harder or ask the rear paddler(s) to slow down to keep it taut. This does not mean pulling so strongly that everyone else feels they have to keep up. Good communications between all members of the group is the key to success, especially when a more complex towing scenario is carried out.

Drag of line in the water.
Photo: Angus Mackie

Boreray and The Stacs.

Rescue in progress.

Assisted Rescues

I cannot even remember who it was that capsized. We were paddling, as a big group of club members, around the most south-westerly peninsula in Scotland, the Mull of Galloway, a place known for strong tides which meet one another, and also for the swell coming up the Irish Sea and from the Atlantic. The conditions were quite lively with waves of around two metres high reflecting off the vertical rock face and causing a fantastic interference pattern.

Most of the time we were paddling as individuals, looking out for our assigned buddies when we were at the top of the waves. I noticed someone in the water some 50 metres behind me holding onto the end of their kayak. His buddy was in front of me and there was no one else close enough to help. I asked my buddy to stay close and have his towline ready should we need it, to stop us being washed onto the cliff.

When we reached the swimmer, it was fairly obvious that he was not too happy with the situation as his eyes were very wide open and he was screaming. The noise of the breaking water all around was pretty loud and I had to shout quite strongly to be heard. After calming him enough so that he could focus on my instructions, I rescued him, a simple affair.

It was at this point I realised that, in this situation, everything close to the centre of the kayak is moving up and down at the same time. As long as the casualty stays close to the centre of rotation of the rescue, there is less chance of the rescuer being capsized.

When we returned to the group in the calm water around the point, many of the others thought that the rescue was extreme and that there was no way that they could have completed it safely. They felt that they didn't yet have the experience and confidence required.

There are many reasons why you may have to perform an assisted rescue. The casualty could be tired, injured, sick or unable to self rescue, or they may just have fallen over while taking a photograph. There are many variables when rescuing another paddler and these are not limited to the condition the casualty is in. It could be the proximity to rocks or any other danger, the mental and physical state of the casualty, the mental and physical state of the rescuer or a combination of all of these.

Sea kayaks have evolved into easy to rescue craft, often with curved and sloped bulkheads just behind the seat so that water doesn't get trapped when you try to empty the kayak, minimum volume cockpits, positive buoyancy provided by the bulkhead and hatch

combination and the addition of deck lines. These enable the rescuer and the casualty to hold on in greater safety than ever before. It is possible for a small rescuer to perform a rescue on a very large casualty without putting any strain on their body whatsoever.

Bulkhead. Photo: Rowland Woollven

GOLDEN RULES OF RESCUE

There are some golden rules to assist with rescues.

APPROACH FROM THE DOWNWIND SIDE

Approach from the downwind side whenever possible.

By doing this, the casualty and their kayak will be blown towards you, the rescuer, rather than you pushed towards, and perhaps over the top of them. Often the speed of closure between you and them is considerable, especially if there is any sea running. Be careful not to surf into the casualty, further compounding the issue.

If you have to approach from upwind, ensure you are in complete control and are not likely to collide with the casualty. Back paddling strongly will slow the kayak enough to give you more control.

Approaching from downwind.

ASSESS THE MENTAL STATE OF THE CASUALTY

Most people who end up in the water are disoriented and not thinking straight. I've found that a good way to reduce their anxiety is to tell them to 'smile', as I take a photograph. It forces them to smile and subconsciously, they are thinking, "If my rescuer can take a photo of me, it can't be that bad a situation". It also buys you a bit of time to gather your thoughts. You have to be completely satisfied that the casualty is calm enough not to capsize you, when you attempt the rescue.

Assess the mental state of the casualty before making contact.

KEEP THE CASUALTY CLOSE

There are many benefits to keeping the casualty close: communication is much easier, you can be more aware of their condition, the rolling moment is reduced to almost zero which is particularly important when there is a choppy sea running, and there is less travelling for the casualty when it is time to get back into the cockpit. If the casualty holds onto your kayak close to the cockpit, they can assist in the rescue, especially if they are on the same side as their own kayak. Their kayak is moved away from them, then back past them and they can stay in the same position relative to the rescuer.

If you don't keep the casualty close, for example, if the casualty is at the end of your kayak, communication will be almost impossible. There is also a higher chance of you being capsized, due to the increased leverage applied at the end of the kayak. The casualty wrapping their legs and arms around the kayak makes this effect more severe and should be avoided.

Placing the casualty at the stern of their kayak, so that they are able to assist in pushing it down while you are emptying the water, is also not good because it puts a lot of pressure on the boat and they are a long way from you. There is also a greater chance of the casualty letting go of their kayak and there is no easy method of reuniting them, especially in a wind or tidal flow.

The casualty close to the cockpit.

THE CASUALTY MUST PLAY A PART IN THEIR RESCUE

By being an active participant, rather than a passive bystander, the casualty is more positive about what is happening. By training to be a casualty (i.e. practising rescues both as a rescuer and as a casualty) it is easier to understand the rescuer's tasks including any difficulties that may occur.

TRIAGE

Whenever there is more than one casualty, or possible casualties, triage must be performed. Originating from French and meaning to 'sort' or 'sift', the concept was probably first used during the Napoleonic wars where the idea was to maximise the number of survivors. For us though, it is more a process of sorting through and prioritising our actions.

1. Assess the situation. What is the problem? What are your resources – who in the group could participate in the rescue? (In order to keep it simple in the following examples it is assumed that there is only one rescuer.)

2. Stabilise the group's situation. Make sure that everyone takes action to ensure that they don't become another casualty. This might be as simple as asking those that aren't able to help in the rescue to land on the nearby beach, wait in an eddy, or hold their position close to the casualties by paddling gently into wind.

3. Stabilise the casualty's situation. If there is more than one casualty, assess the situation and prioritise anyone in immediate danger. Either rescue them (if this is just as quick) or take action to stabilise their situation. For example if one casualty is 100m offshore (and therefore in no 'immediate' danger) and the other about to be washed onto the rocks, you would have to either perform a quick rescue or tow him clear of the rocks.

4. Prioritise who gets rescued. As the situation is now relatively stable, this would be in order of effectiveness and speed of the whole rescue. For example if there is only one rescuer and there are two casualties, one who has lost his paddle and one who is in the water, the most effective rescue would be to retrieve the paddle before it disappears, give it to the casualty before they capsize, and then deal with the person in the water.

WET EXIT

The first thing you need to do after a wet exit is to orientate yourself. You move to the bow of your kayak with your paddle and, keeping off to one side, rotate the kayak into the upright position.

The rescuer can then approach and easily hold onto your kayak, while issuing instructions. The rescuer is in charge of everything from this point onwards and you must do as you are told. You must not let go of your kayak nor try to grab the rescuer, as this will most likely result in the rescuer backing off until you calm down. You must keep close to the rescuer's cockpit, as from this position it is possible to be of assistance.

Casualty at the bow with their paddle.

If you become separated from your kayak, and still have your paddle, put your paddle vertically in the air, always turning to face the rescuer. If you have dropped your paddle, put one hand in the air and keep it moving as you face the rescuer.

Paddle in air, the signal for 'everyone come to my position'. Photo: Rowland Woollven

LOOKING AFTER THE PADDLES

Being constantly aware of the paddles, and where they are, is essential for a successful sea kayak rescue. It is highly likely that the rescuer's focus during the rescue will be on the rescue and casualty, and not the paddles. As with everything else, there are several options.

It is unwise, however, to give the paddles to the casualty to look after (unless in certain extreme circumstances), as their state of mind is probably not conducive to making sure they are still holding onto them when the rescuer asks for the paddles back at the end.

Where are the paddles? ... Oops!

ACROSS THE RESCUER'S DECK

The best place for the paddles is across the rescuer's deck. In this position, they will move around slowly and it is easy to keep a check on them as they are close to both the rescuer and the casualty. Because they are trapped between the kayak and the rescuer's body, there is less chance that they will drift off.

Paddles across the deck in front of the rescuer.

UNDER THE DECK ELASTICS

By sliding the blade of the paddle fully under the deck elastic on the side away from the casualty and their kayak, the paddle(s) are close to the rescuer and are easy to remove when the rescue is completed. Care has to be taken to push the paddle through far enough otherwise there is a risk that the paddle will float away. Getting the paddle under the elastic can be awkward to start with, so having the elastic raised off the deck by a few millimetres will help. You can either lift the elastic with your hand or prepare for this in advance by tying an overhand knot at each side of the elastic you will push the paddle under.

Blade held under a deck elastic.

PADDLE LEASH

This is a piece of cord or elastic, with a clip on one end to attach to the kayak and a piece of velcro on the other that wraps around the paddle. There are many types available; from a coiled surfboard leash-type, to a length of tape with sewn ends, to a simple piece of cord tied onto the boat and paddle.

A downside of paddle leashes is that they encourage the paddler to let go of the paddle and trust in the leash to keep the paddle from floating off. All too often I have seen paddles floating away from the rescue site, as the rescuer is so involved in the action of the rescue that they have forgotten to keep a lookout for all of the other pieces of equipment.

PADDLE PARK

The paddle park is similar to the leash. The difference is that the paddle is only attached to it when a rescue is in progress. A paddle park is usually a loop of rope or bungee attached to the deck lines of the kayak. A contact towline fitted to the deck can be used as a paddle park, by clipping one end around the paddle and back onto the line.

Contact towline used as a paddle park.

Another option is to extend the deck lines beyond the fitting closest to the cockpit and add a clip onto the end – this could also double as a contact tow. One benefit of using a system such as this to secure the paddle(s) during a rescue, is that there is less chance of them drifting off as the attachment is more secure. A drawback is that the paddles need to be released from the system before they can be used.

Whichever method you choose to use to manage the paddles during the rescue, you need to check continuously that they are still attached and not floating off.

ASSISTED RESCUES

These are the most used methods of assisted rescue, there isn't one that is always right, and all of them have a place. Which one you choose will depend on the circumstances and the position you find yourself in.

CLIMB IN, PUMP OUT

Just flip the kayak upright and climb in. It really can be this simple and there is no need to lift the kayak from the water to empty it. This method is especially useful when on expedition and paddling with fully laden kayaks. It is also a good way to rescue a double, as it puts much less strain on the rescuer.

After your capsize, you turn the kayak upright. The rescuer approaches from downwind and comes alongside to stabilise the kayak, which will be pretty full of water. They will hold onto the deck lines on both sides, just forwards of the cockpit. You climb back into the cockpit and start the long, slow job of pumping the cockpit dry.

I've found that short strokes with the pump are more efficient than long, full strokes, as it doesn't work the shoulders as much. When emptied, put the spraydeck back on and continue the journey.

Sitting in a kayak after climbing back in (note how much water is in the kayak).

The casualty ends up spending much less time immersed in the water but much more time sitting in a kayak that is full of water. If not dressed for full immersion, the casualty will be cold and need to get dry and warmed up. Often this will mean going ashore at the first opportunity. It could also be that the day has to be cut short and camp set up, depending on how cold the casualty has become.

X RESCUE (A.K.A. T RESCUE)

The casualty holding onto their kayak and paddle until the rescuer is ready.

This is the classic rescue when on the sea. You turn your kayak up the right way and move to the bow. The rescuer approaches close enough, ideally from downwind, to allow you to hold onto their kayak close to the cockpit. This keeps all of the weight close to the centre of rotation. It is important that you maintain hold of your kayak.

The rescuer slides the kayak onto their deck.

When stable in this position, the rescuer takes the paddles and secures them using one of the methods described above. Only then will the rescuer hold onto your kayak, allowing you to release your grip.

Creating a ramp to ease the slide by edging the kayak.

The rescuer now slides (no lifting) your kayak onto their deck. Due to the upsweep of the bow, this is an easy movement and does not stress the body unduly. By edging slightly towards the casualty's kayak, a ramp is created thus easing the slide even more.

EMPTYING THE KAYAK

Once the kayak is on the rescuer's deck and up the right way, there are several options to empty the kayak. It does not matter which of these methods you use as it comes down to personal preference and what you have practised most.

EDGE METHOD

Holding onto the bow end toggle, fully commit your body weight to the toggle as you first edge, then lean away from the kayak to be emptied. The result is that the casualty's kayak will invert and empty without any other action. This method does require a lot of commitment and relies on the casualty allowing your kayak to go completely onto its edge. Recovering from this almost-capsized position is awkward as you have to turn the casualty's kayak up the right way, at the same time as you sit back upright. Spending time practising will bring success, even in turbulent water.

The edge method.

ROLL METHOD

Holding onto the bow end toggle, slide the kayak onto your deck and transfer your grip to the deck lines. Move the kayak until the front hatch is at the level of your spraydeck and then invert it by holding onto the deck line on the side closest to you and gripping onto the keel over the top of the kayak. This means that the kayak rolls towards you and you will have better control of its movement.

When it is inverted, put both hands onto the keel line and edge slightly away from the side the kayak is on. This edging will lift the cockpit clear of the water and allow the cockpit to drain completely. When the water has drained from the upturned kayak, right it by turning it towards you again. At the same time, sit back upright and slide it back into the water.

The roll method.

CROOK OF ARM METHOD

As above, hold the toggle and pull until the kayak is at the hatch. This time rather than turning the kayak over, hold onto the deck line with the hand closest to the casualty's cockpit and with the other hand reach over until you can feel the keel. Pull the keel towards you and rotate the kayak until it is resting in the crook of your arm closest to the cockpit. This method lifts the kayak well clear of the water and is a good option if you are strong.

The crook of arm method.

CURL

If, in addition to the cockpit, the bow or stern compartments become completely filled with water, either because a hatch cover has been lost, or the kayak has been damaged, there is a fairly straightforward method of emptying the water to allow a repair. The rescuer does not have to lift anything, as the casualty does all the work.

First, with the bow compartment flooded, the rescuer comes alongside facing in the same direction as your kayak and holds onto your stern. With the kayak secured, you move to the other side of the rescuer's kayak, away from yours, and give the rescuer the paddles to look after. You now reach over the rescuer's kayak, and as the rescuer pushes down on the stern, thereby raising the bow, you get hold of the front hatch rim.

Put both hands into the hatch with the palms facing upwards against the underside of the deck and place your elbows on the front deck of the rescuer's kayak. Lean back keeping your elbows at 90°. This slow movement lifts the kayak gently, and with practice it can be levered onto the deck of the rescuer's kayak. Allow it to drain before the rescuer turns it back up the right way.

The same technique can be applied in the case of the stern compartment being flooded, although this presents less of a problem as the day hatch still provides buoyancy and the cockpit doesn't fill with water to the same extent as if the bow hatch floods.

THE CURL:

The curl.
Photo: Rowland
Woollven

PUTTING THE KAYAK BACK INTO THE WATER

When putting the kayak back into the water, the most important thing is to keep hold of it, keep it under control and manoeuvre it into an appropriate position to allow the casualty to re-enter their cockpit.

Putting the kayak back into the water. Photo: Joe Hughes

SECURING THE CASUALTY'S KAYAK

Position the casualty's kayak facing in the opposite direction to yours. By holding the deck lines on either side of the kayak close to the cockpit, you can exert a wide grip, allowing much better use of the whole body to stabilise everything.

The centreline of the deck should be directly below your armpit as this allows a greater area of contact. Once in this

A wide grip, holding onto the deck lines.

position, lower the head and perform a 'crunch' with your stomach muscles, pulling your knees towards your chest.

This stabilises the whole raft and makes a very secure platform for the casualty to climb onto. One major benefit to holding on in this way, is the ability to see the casualty throughout the rescue process and even help them if they are struggling to get back in. The hand that is between the kayaks can let go of the deck line, and by reaching across the casualty's kayak, can assist by holding onto their buoyancy aid, leg or whatever else is available.

In the position ready to perform the 'crunch'.

The weight of your body together with the 'crunch' will hold the kayaks together. As soon as the casualty is back in their cockpit, move the grip back onto the deck line to ensure the raft is stable.

In this position, you can also assist in refitting the spraydeck. The casualty puts the rear of the spraydeck on. While continuing to hold onto the deck line, your other hand can now stretch the spraydeck forwards enough that the casualty can flip the lip over the cockpit rim. With practice, it is possible for the rescuer to refit a very tight neoprene spraydeck without assistance from the casualty.

The rescuer giving a helping hand.

If, for whatever reason, the kayaks are facing the same direction, set up exactly the same way. It will be more difficult to see and help the casualty but still possible. Helping with the spraydeck will be much more difficult from this position.

The rescuer helping the casualty with their spraydeck.

GETTING BACK IN

There are many ways for the casualty to get back into the safety of the cockpit; some require athletic movement and strength, while others rely on the strength of the rescuer. Whatever method you prefer it is good to practise many different ways to get in or help someone else get back in. This will allow you to make a better choice when faced with a situation that is perhaps different to those seen and practised previously.

THE HEEL HOOK

The rescuer holds onto your kayak as described above. Facing towards the rescuer, put the foot of the leg that is closest to the bow into the cockpit. Secure your foot below the cockpit rim. When this is done, move your hands onto the top of the rear deck.

Reach across the kayak behind the cockpit with the hand on the same side as the foot used, and hold onto the rescuer's deck lines or side of the kayak. Now straighten the leg in the cockpit and at the same time pull with the arm holding the deck line. Your body will rise from the water, rotate and lie face down on the rear deck.

Continue the rotation using almost a corkscrew motion, and your buttocks will end up in the seat. As the rotation is towards the rescuer, stability is not much of an issue. It is then a matter of putting the other leg into the cockpit, removing the last of the water and refitting the spraydeck.

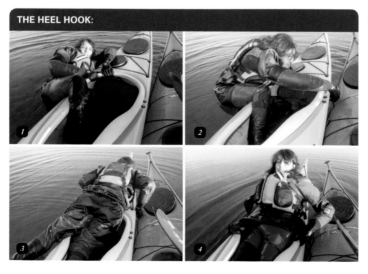

THE HEEL HOOK:

The heel hook.

THE BELLY FLOP

If you are strong and athletic, the belly flop re-entry works well. The rescuer stabilises the kayaks as before, you hold onto your kayak, one hand on your side of the cockpit rim and the other on the other side of the kayak. By combining a leg-kick with an arm-pull and push, you will lift your body from the water and end up on the back deck of your kayak, belly down.

Roll over until you can drop your buttocks into the seat. This method is straightforward but can place quite a bit of strain on the rescuer, especially if you are heavy.

The belly flop.

TWIST AND DROP

If you are light and athletic, it is possible to start in the same position as for the belly flop but twist at the same time as you lift your body from the water. This allows you to drop straight into your cockpit and you won't spend any time on the rear deck.

Twist and drop. Photo: Joe Hughes

MODIFIED HEEL HOOK

When the casualty is between the kayaks, it is still possible to get back in, but other techniques will be needed and it isn't easy. The modified heel hook works best in this situation.

You are in the water between the two kayaks facing the rescuer who (in this description) is on your right, holding onto the kayaks as before. You place your left arm over your kayak, hold onto the deck line furthest away and lift your right leg onto the rescuer's front deck. As you roll into a face-down position, lift your body from the water and onto the rear deck of your kayak using both your leg and arms to do so. You should be completely clear of the water. Continue the rotation until you can drop into the seat.

If you change the direction of your roll from the face-down position, you will find it slightly more awkward to get into the seat but not impossible.

This method places considerably less strain on the rescuer than the conventional heel hook method.

Although the modified heel hook feels safe due to starting between the kayaks, in very turbulent water there is a high possibility of receiving impact and crush injuries from the kayaks, as they move around.

MODIFIED HEEL HOOK:

The modified heel hook.

THE LADDER

When the casualty is very large in comparison to the rescuer, the ladder technique works every time. Both kayaks are facing the same direction; the rescuer sits upright and holds onto the deck lines on both sides of the kayak but does not lean over the deck or lower the head.

Make your way to the rear of the rescuer's kayak, push down with your hands and due to your combined weight, the rear of the kayak sinks and you are able to ease yourself onto the back deck in a prone position. Moving towards your own cockpit, the buoyancy that is released as your weight comes off the rescuer's kayak helps lift you out of the water. At this point, move into a sitting position astride your kayak and then start putting your legs into your cockpit. By moving your weight across to your kayak, the strain on the rescuer is reduced to practically nothing. This is a fantastic method of entering the kayak if you are tired as well as heavy, as it does not require a great amount of strength by either person to perform.

THE LADDER:

The ladder. Photo: Duncan Barwise

FEET FIRST

The feet first method came about through a series of experiments many years ago into what was possible, and I have since developed it in response to a client who has a problem with her legs going into spasm when she tries to put any pressure on them. She was unable to easily get back into her kayak by any of the other methods so I resurrected this fun technique.

The kayaks face opposite directions and the rescuer holds onto the casualty's kayak as before. Lie on your back in the water, put both feet across the cockpit area. Hold the cockpit with the hand that is towards the bow, and with the other hand, hold the deck line behind the cockpit. You should be looking at the sky. Now put your head into the water and arch your back while pulling the kayak, your bottom should end up in the seat.

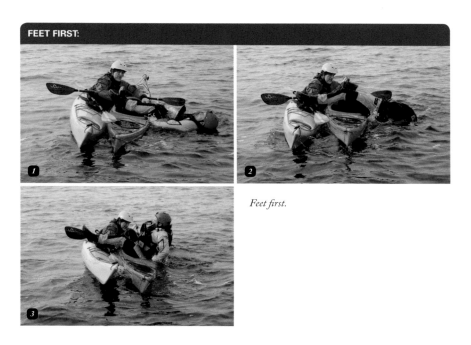

Feet first.

STIRRUP

The stirrup is a piece of line with a rigid step of plastic tubing. The tube keeps a space to allow the foot to go in easily and the overall length should be around 40cm. Keep it in the buoyancy aid until needed. An alternative is to use the 'dog-lead' tow to fashion a makeshift stirrup. This takes a bit longer but works equally as well.

The rescuer connects the stirrup to their contact towline and places it over the casualty's kayak, clear of the cockpit. The bottom of the stirrup should be about 30cm below the hull of the kayak, to be most efficient. As you put your weight into the stirrup, both kayaks are pulled together and stabilised significantly. Stand up, holding onto your kayak, this will bring you out of the water, then you can lie on your deck or turn around and sit into your cockpit.

The stirrup ready to be used.

THINGS TO AVOID WHEN PERFORMING A RESCUE

◎ Approaching the casualty before assessing the whole situation.

◎ Becoming too focused on the casualty during the rescue, to the detriment of yourself and others.

◎ Shouting – this always makes you sound frightened or angry. Learn to project your voice and talk loudly.

◎ Turning to the side and lifting a kayak onto your deck. Your spine is not designed to work this way.

◎ Dropping a kayak onto your spraydeck. There is a risk that it will cut the spraydeck material and damage the cockpit rim.

ESKIMO RESCUES

These come under the heading of assisted rescues because a paddling partner is required to perform them. There are various approaches but all require the casualty to be able to hold their breath for long enough to allow completion.

After capsizing, do not wet exit but remain in your kayak. Bend forwards and give the kayak a hug, with your face close to the cockpit. In this position, use your hands to bang on the hull several times to attract attention. Then turn your hands 90° so that the thumbs move along the kayak and sweep in a back and forward motion describing a big arc of a circle.

Hands at 90°.

This gives you a better chance of feeling the rescuer's kayak if you can't see it, and your hands are less likely to be trapped or crushed between the kayaks.

Making contact close to the casualty's hands.

When the rescuer approaches, they should travel towards the hands, steadily with purpose, but aim to miss them. Approach parallel to the casualty's kayak, whether from the front or the back does not matter. The rescuer's kayak should make contact with your kayak within reach of your hands. The rescuer should keep paddling gently as this will ensure their kayak moves towards your hands while keeping contact with the hull of your upturned kayak.

When you feel the end of the rescuer's kayak presented, transfer both your hands to it. By lifting your head, it is possible to get a breath of air and slow the next part of the rescue. Driving the knee closest to the rescuer's kayak and dropping the other introduces rotation to your upturned kayak. This rotation should be continued with the body. Keep your head in the water for as long as possible. Finally, sit up and rearrange yourself in the cockpit, gathering any equipment that has floated off.

If the rescuer approaches at 90° to the casualty's kayak, the speed and angle need to be absolutely correct, as a slight variation would result in the rescuer's kayak being out of reach or in the rescuer crashing into the casualty's kayak. Approaching at a more acute angle from either end gives the casualty more options for taking hold of the rescuer's kayak (bow, alongside, paddle or stern).

THE ESKIMO RESCUE:

The Eskimo rescue.

When I was much younger, the club I was a member of ran winter training courses in the swimming pool and, when spring arrived, we transferred our skills to the sea. I remember one course where a father and son came along and were successful in everything, especially anything that involved being inverted. They were both keen divers.

When the time came to go outside, we paddled around the breakwater at Ardrossan and once in the shelter, I heard a thumping sound. Checking around the group, I realised that one of us was missing. Taking everyone with me, we retraced our track and on the outside of the wall, we found a kayak upside-down with hands beating on the hull and then waving back and forward just as we had practised in the swimming pool. A flurry of paddle strokes brought me into contact with the hand closest and we made a successful recovery.

This focused my coaching and I started to teach that an Eskimo rescue can only be carried out when paddling alongside, or at least close, to your buddy. If you notice your paddling partner starting to wobble a bit, position yourself just behind and off to one side. This puts you in a perfect position to respond to a capsize and allows a quick and successful Eskimo rescue to take place.

RE-ENTER AND ESKIMO RESCUE

This is a nice form of (almost) self rescue. Once you have wet exited wait until the rescuer is close by, then seat yourself back into the cockpit of your inverted kayak while holding the end of the rescuer's kayak. Once in, and with your feet braced on the footrest, continue as for the Eskimo rescue described above. This is a very quick rescue and only needs a quick pump out of the cockpit to complete it.

RE-ENTER AND ESKIMO RESCUE:

Re-enter and Eskimo rescue.

'HAND OF GOD' AND SCOOP

These two rescues are very similar, the main difference being that the Hand of God is aimed at righting someone who is trapped in their kayak, while the scoop is more about getting an injured casualty back into their kayak.

HAND OF GOD

You come alongside the upturned kayak and, laying your chest across the casualty's hull, reach over and hold onto the cockpit rim with the hand nearest the bow. With your other hand, hold onto the casualty's buoyancy aid shoulder strap or another strong point. Due to the chance of injuring the casualty, perhaps dislocating their shoulder, it is **not** a good idea to hold onto either their hand or arm.

Put both your elbows onto the edge of the kayak and push down while simultaneously pulling both your hands towards your shoulders. The casualty and their kayak should turn up the right way. This obviously works best if the rescuer is bigger than the casualty, but with practice, it is possible for a small person to rescue a much larger one.

An important consideration is that if the casualty is unable to exit their kayak and has been underwater for some time, they will be struggling. It is therefore worthwhile practising the Hand of God rescue with both an inert, relaxed casualty and a struggling, fighting one.

THE 'HAND OF GOD':

The 'Hand of God'.

SCOOP

The scoop is a useful technique for righting an injured, or even unconscious, casualty. The method is the same as for the Hand of God, but first you must put the casualty back into their kayak.

If the casualty is injured, turn their kayak onto its side and help them slide all the way into their cockpit. They will be in a lying down position with the kayak still on its side, not sitting up.

If the casualty is large, and is able to, ask them to turn to face their kayak and hug it. This reduces the amount of leverage necessary and makes the work involved in righting them much easier.

Proceed as for the Hand of God.

If faced with an unconscious casualty (a situation which is fortunately rare), you must ensure that their airway is not compromised further when you put them in the cockpit. The buoyancy aid can constrict the chest, especially if it rests on the cockpit rim. If they are face down in the cockpit, their head will roll forward due to the angle created by the buoyancy aid, the back of the cockpit and the slope of the body as it goes into the kayak. This 'face-down' position is both good and bad. The good is that anything in the mouth can drain, so there is less chance of the airway becoming compromised. The bad is that it is more difficult to check for breathing and the airway will need careful management.

The scoop can also be used to rescue a tired paddler. Note that there will always be water in the kayak after turning it upright.

THE SCOOP:

The scoop.

TOWED RESCUE

When performing a rescue close to an area of turbulence which you don't want to be in, or if there is a likelihood of drifting or being blown or pushed onto rocks, then a towed rescue should take place. The towing is carried out by a third person.

The rescuer approaches the casualty and is the person in charge. When the rescuer decides that they are getting too close to the obstruction, they instruct another paddler to clip their tow onto their kayak to hold the position. The aim is to stabilise the situation and stop any drifting towards the area of danger.

The paddler towing must not pull as hard as they can, as this will make the rescue much more difficult to perform. They are simply there to hold the position.

A towed rescue.

SWIMMER RESCUES

Sometimes it may be safer to get the swimmer to safety and then go back for the kayak.

STERN DECK CARRY

If the situation demands, it is possible to make progress with a casualty on the back deck of your kayak. Stabilise your kayak while the casualty climbs on, this is most effectively done by sculling. Once across the back deck, the casualty turns and lies along the kayak with their head close to your back. In this position they can hold onto you and keep their chest on the widest part of the kayak. With both legs lying flat on the surface of the water, the stability is reasonable, with little drag. There is less risk of hypothermia than if the swimmer remains in the water.

With a swimmer on the back deck.

TOWING A SWIMMER

The scenario: a kayaker has entered a rock gully, capsized and wet exited.

The rescuer, with a towline attached to their kayak, advances towards the casualty. A third kayaker is performing the tow and keeps the line taut. The casualty grabs hold of the rescuer's kayak, keeping a firm grip on their own kayak and paddle, and lets the rescuer know when they are ready. The rescuer commands the tow kayaker to paddle away from the rock. The rescuer needs to stay upright while supporting the casualty and, if possible, assist by paddling too.

Casualty holding rescuer's kayak and their own kayak.

Once clear of the immediate danger, a normal rescue can take place. The tow kayak stays attached until the rescue is complete and the tow is only released when the rescuer asks for it.

This rescue obviously requires a lot of teamwork as well as good communication between the group members. It is important that the casualty holds onto their kayak and paddle throughout the rescue, as gathering up the equipment would add to the difficulty and could result in the casualty spending substantially more time in the water.

As with a towed rescue, the rescuer is in charge of everything. The towline is adjusted to a length that allows the tow kayak to be far enough away to let them paddle well, but close enough so that they can hear any commands.

There are variations on the theme. The rescuer approaches backwards, which allows them to apply more power after the pick up. The tow kayaker approaches forwards, this lets them see what is going on and when to paddle. As with most things, there are associated benefits and drawbacks.

THE RAFT

A 'raft' is when two or more kayaks 'raft up' to provide stability. The kayaks are brought together facing the same direction and the paddles are placed across the front of the cockpits, close to the paddlers' bodies and held there with the elbows over the shaft and pushing down.

There are a couple of issues with the raft technique. The first is the speed at which the raft drifts. Due to the increased windage, a raft of two kayaks will drift much quicker that a single kayak, and a single kayak will drift much quicker than a person in the water.

Anyone not directly involved in the rescue should stay close to the scene, on the downwind side of the rescue. To maintain their position, they should face their kayak into the wind and paddle steadily.

Two-kayak raft.

The second issue is that in a choppy sea, the kayaks will be banging together and there is a chance of injury if attempting to retrieve anything from between the kayaks.

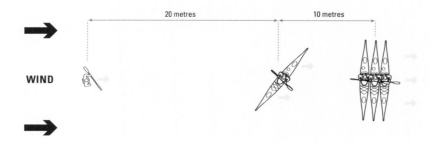

Person in water, single kayak and drifting raft all drifting at different rates.

The other kayakers in the group holding their position relative to the rescue.

Eskimo roll in the rain.

Self Rescue

I was leading a group in the tide race at Kylerhea on Skye and the emphasis of the session was on personal performance. The flow was running at around seven knots with a twenty-five knot wind opposing, resulting in some fairly big waves. One of the group capsized and wet exited. I performed a deep water rescue and as the casualty was getting back into the kayak, I saw a wave breaking. I held on around the casualty's waist and we were both thrown upside down, then back upright, as the wave continued its push to depletion.

I was now well and truly stuck in my kayak as the wave had turned the casualty's kayak at right angles across my back deck. I turned around, and to move it off my deck and back into the water I had to take both thighs from their locked-in position ... and that is when the next wave threw us both in again.

This time, I was pulled straight out of the cockpit by the force of the water and when I came to the surface, I realised that we were both still close together. I quickly re-entered and rolled and will never forget the look on the face of my fellow casualty when I arrived to rescue again.

The remainder of the group started to gather around as we paddled into the shelter of the eddy and I was disappointed that not one of them had taken any photographs of the incident.

The ability to recover from a capsize and continue on a journey is unique to the kayak and sets it apart from all other types of boat in the world. Other than a lifeboat, it is the only craft on the ocean that can be righted by its crew without external equipment, without the risk of serious damage and without having to exit.

THE ESKIMO ROLL

The Eskimo roll was born out of necessity in the icy waters of the far north where kayaks evolved. Exiting the kayak and spending any amount of time in the water would have resulted in certain death.

It is the ultimate self rescue and there are many books and videos on the technique. My recommendations are *Kayak Rolling, the Black Art Demystified* by Loel Collins, Pesda Press and *Sea Kayak with Gordon Brown, Vol. 3 Rolling Clinic*, Sunart Media.

PERFORMING A SELF RESCUE

Besides the roll, there are many other self-rescue methods. Even when you can roll, there are good reasons for developing the ability to self rescue, as someone with a 'bombproof' roll can nevertheless end up in the water, as illustrated in the story above. When paddling solo, or if everyone ends up in the water at the same time and you are not close to another kayak, it could be the only way to get out of trouble. In some circumstances, you may need to swim from the shore to avoid a dangerous launch, a process I have described in the box at the end of the chapter.

As with most techniques, self rescue should be practised in a safe location before progressing onto the sea and the conditions in which you normally paddle. What works on flat water, does not always have the same effect in a heaving sea or tide race.

HOLDING THE KAYAK WITH YOUR FEET

After you have exited your kayak, ensure that every piece of equipment is where it should be and hold onto your inverted kayak. The most efficient way, so that both your hands are free, is to keep one leg in the cockpit and hook the other foot over the side of the kayak furthest away from you.

Keeping hold of your kayak with your feet.
Photo: Rowland Woollven

RE-ENTER AND ROLL

This is the quickest method of getting back into the kayak but it does leave quite a bit of water in the cockpit, which will have to be pumped out.

Begin in the water with the kayak on its side and face the cockpit opening. With one hand, hold the paddle against the upper side of the kayak and the cockpit rim at the same time. Swing your legs into the cockpit and simultaneously, with your other hand, hold the cockpit rim below the legs.

At this point, take a deep breath as the kayak will turn completely upside down. Pull the kayak onto you so that your feet go beyond the footrest as this ensures a correct position for the set-up. Put your feet onto the footrest and then engage your knees, or thighs, under the deck. Move the lower hand from the cockpit rim onto the paddle, which should still be in the other hand and on the cockpit rim. Now perform a roll.

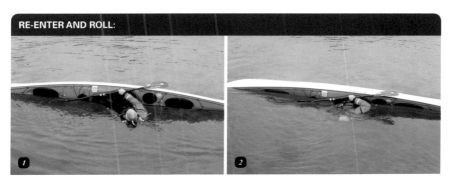

RE-ENTER AND ROLL:

Re-enter and roll. Photo: Kate Duffus

If concerned, try extending the paddle to gain extra leverage. This can sometimes make all the difference, as the cockpit will be considerably full of water.

PUSH TO EMPTY

For any method other than re-entry and roll, empty the water out of the cockpit as much as possible before starting to self rescue. This ensures the kayak will be more stable when you get back in the cockpit. As with everything else, practise until your chosen way becomes easy.

Secure the paddle somewhere and with the kayak upside down, hold onto it approximately 30cm from the bow. Have your legs vertical in the water as a strong kick downwards is required. Take a deep breath. Scissor kick and push the kayak up above your head and flip it upright. This empties most of the water from the cockpit.

When you push upwards, it is likely that your head will go under the water so a good breath is advantageous. Timing is critical. If the push and flip are not synchronised, the kayak will end up back in the water still inverted, or upright still full of water.

Push and kick to empty the kayak. Photo: Rowland Woollven

PADDLE LEVER EMPTY

Facing the inverted kayak from the front, place the paddle over your shoulder (the weaker one, if you have one) with the blade flat on the water surface, and extend it as far away from your body as possible. The elbow on this side should be bent at approximately 90°. Open your other hand and make a 'crook' and put the bow of the kayak into this, don't hold it. Then simultaneously pull down on the paddle while pushing up on the kayak. The kayak will lift from the water, the water will empty from the cockpit and it will turn itself upright when it has emptied.

Emptying the kayak, using the paddle as a lever. Photo: Rowland Woollven

If the kayak is loaded, lifting the kayak becomes untenable and the best option is to turn the kayak up the right way and pump out when back in the cockpit.

As the paddler sees it. Photo: Kate Duffus

BELLY FLOP ONTO BACK DECK

This method requires good coordination. Hold onto the cockpit rim close to your body. With the other hand, reach for the far side of the kayak as far as possible towards the stern. This gives a good stable base to work from.

Lie flat on the surface, kick down with both feet at the same time (dolphin kick) while simultaneously pushing down on the cockpit rim and pulling the kayak under your body.

If you find it difficult, it may be because your legs are too vertical in the water. This makes the kayak rotate towards you, places pressure on your hand or paddle and makes climbing out almost impossible.

Hand position. Photo: Kate Duffus

The belly flop. Photo: Rowland Woollven

If you move closer to the stern where there is less buoyancy in the kayak, it will be easier to push below the surface but ... there will also be less stability once you are on top of the kayak. A bigger, heavier paddler can push down near the stern of the kayak and completely submerge it allowing an easier swim onto the deck.

TWIST AND DROP

For the light and agile this is as described in the previous chapter except that no one is holding your kayak.

LOG ROLL

When in the belly-down position across the rear deck, the quickest and most efficient method of getting back into the seat is the log roll. Keep your weight low, roll towards the front of the kayak and drop your bottom into the seat. It takes a very small amount of time and with practice becomes one fluid movement.

Log roll. Photo: Kate Duffus

THE STRADDLE

From the 'belly flop onto back deck' position, while still lying on your stomach, swivel around so that your legs end up on either side of the kayak. Then sit up, finishing legs straight and feet on the surface of the water. Next put your bottom into the seat, followed by one foot and leg. Put this foot onto the footrest, brace inside the kayak and then put the other leg in.

Sat up in balance on the rear deck.
Photo: Rowland Woollven

Free hands to pump out.
Photo: Rowland Woollven

BUOYANCY AID PROBLEMS

Often the buoyancy aid will hinder getting onto the rear deck, especially when there is a lot of cargo carried in the front pockets. Loosening the front fastening can help but is perhaps not the smartest thing to do.

Many women find that the combination of body shape, less strength, and the bulk of the buoyancy aid make it difficult to get onto the back of the kayak. In this case, it is worthwhile trying the 'feet first' method.

SELF RESCUE WITH A PADDLE FLOAT

Paddle floats come in many shapes and sizes and with different types of buoyancy.

SELECTING A PADDLE FLOAT

With a rigid foam float, there is nothing to do other than put it on the paddle, but it is difficult to stow so has to be attached to the deck of the kayak. On the rear deck it will impede towing and most entry and exit methods; on the front deck, it will always be in sight. No matter where it is stowed, it will catch the wind enough to make the kayak more difficult to handle. The advantage is that it is always ready for use.

Inflatable paddle floats can be rolled up and secured under deck elastics, behind the seat, or even carried in the rear pocket of the buoyancy aid. The downside is that it needs to be inflated before it can give support. Doing this in cold water, having just capsized, wet exited and struggling to get a breath, is hard work and the difficulties should not be underestimated.

A float with two chambers seems to work most efficiently, especially when learning the skills involved, as it gives greater flotation, but it does take more time to inflate. There are gas-inflatable models available with either one or two chambers. These work well and can be inflated orally as well, which means that for training purposes, it is possible to inflate through the mouthpiece keeping the gas inflator for that real situation.

A selection of paddle floats.

Rigid float stowed on deck.

Inflatable paddle float stowed behind the seat.

Both types have a 'pocket' where the paddle blade is inserted and secured by either a clip or drawstring. This stops the paddle blade pulling out of the pocket and makes the float more reliable in operation. The chamber is then inflated to give positive buoyancy. If one chamber only is inflated, the paddle float works a bit like a weight as well, due to the water contained within the other chamber. This ballast can stop the float lifting from the water and although there is less buoyancy, there will be more chance of success.

Paddle float with pocket.

An alternative to a purpose-made paddle float is to use a large water bag, partially filled with water, and then inflated by blowing air into it. It works the same way.

One very well thought out paddle float is the FourPlay from Northwater. It is a folding paddle float, which can be used as an insulating pad or chair. The paddle can be inserted from either end, making it even quicker to deploy.

PADDLE FLOAT STABILITY

If the paddle float is on the paddle and inflated, you can achieve a good stable position by pulling the paddle shaft into your stomach below the buoyancy aid. Lean forwards and put all your weight onto the shaft while favouring the side the paddle float is on. By placing your elbows onto the paddle shaft, it is possible to use both hands on a stirrup pump to empty the remaining water from the kayak.

RE-ENTER AND PADDLE FLOAT ROLL

Secure the paddle float on the blade that will be towards the front of the kayak and inflate it. Everything else is the same as for the re-enter and roll method described above.

Setting up for the re-enter and roll using the paddle float.
Photo: Kate Duffus

PUSH TO EMPTY, PADDLE FLOAT ASSISTED

Place the paddle float on the paddle blade and inflate it. Put the paddle between your legs with the float close in front of your body. Proceed as for 'push to empty'. The added buoyancy helps keep your head from submerging.

The lever technique can also be used with a paddle float.

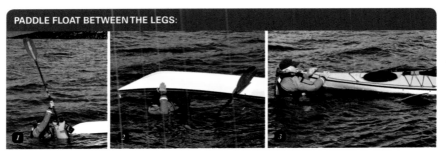

PADDLE FLOAT BETWEEN THE LEGS:

Paddle float between the legs. Photo: Joe Hughes

GETTING BACK IN USING A PADDLE FLOAT

With a paddle float, the method is essentially the same as the belly flop followed by the log roll. There are a couple of different ways you can secure the paddle to stabilise the kayak during the manoeuvre:

1. With one hand, hold onto your paddle and the deck line behind the cockpit. This will be easier if you keep your thumb over the top of the shaft and curl the fingers around the line. Make sure the blade is fully on the rear deck and hold it at right angles.

2. Push the paddle below the deck line on the side from which you are entering. This ensures a more secure placement, but there is a risk of damaging the paddle because all the forces are focused onto one small area of the shaft.

Below are a number of variations for getting back into your kayak using a paddle float.

Holding the paddle shaft and deck line.

Paddle held below deck lines. Photo: Kate Duffus

THE HEEL HOOK WITH A PADDLE FLOAT

The heel hook is described in the previous chapter (*Assisted Rescues*) but instead of a rescuer, you will use a paddle float to provide the extra support needed.

With the hand closest to the stern, hold the paddle onto the deck line with the thumb over the top of the shaft and the fingers curled around the line. Face the kayak and put the foot of the leg that is towards the bow into the cockpit. Secure your foot below the cockpit rim. Reach across the kayak behind the cockpit with the hand on the same side as the foot used (bow hand), and hold onto the deck lines or side of the kayak. Now straighten the leg in the cockpit and at the same time pull with the bow hand. Your body will rise from the water, rotate and lie face down on the rear deck.

Favouring the side the paddle float is on, rotate into a sitting position and get your other leg into the cockpit.

THE HEEL HOOK USING A PADDLE FLOAT:

*The heel hook using a paddle float.
Photo: Rowland Woollven*

FEET FIRST WITH A PADDLE FLOAT

The feet first method is also described in the previous chapter (*Assisted Rescues*). It is a quick way to get back into the cockpit but takes a bit of time to set up.

Put the paddle float onto the paddle and secure it below both deck lines behind the cockpit. Lie on your back in the water, put both feet across the cockpit area. Hold the

Feet first with a paddle float. Photo: Kate Duffus

cockpit with the hand that is towards the bow, and with the other hand, hold the deck line behind the cockpit. You should be looking at the sky. Now put your head into the water and arch your back while pulling the kayak. Your bottom should end up in the seat. Get the legs and feet in, favouring the side the paddle float is on. With practice, it is possible to use this method without a paddle float, but it requires determination to make it work.

REMOVING THE PADDLE AND FLOAT

If the paddle is secured below the deck lines of the kayak, freeing it to remove the paddle float can be a tricky manoeuvre as everything has to be done behind the cockpit. Edging away from the side the paddle is on can help and being supple will help a lot, Once the paddle is removed, deflate the paddle float and stow it in its normal place, unless that is behind the seat.

SWIM AND LAND OR LAUNCH AND SWIM

Being well practised in self rescue techniques is useful if you find yourself in a situation where it is safer to swim to the shore rather than attempt to land in a kayak. It could also be the case that you need to launch the kayak and swim out rather than launch from the shore. This could be somewhere with large boulders or near vertical walls which make the landing / launch area potentially dangerous.

Attempting to do this when it is calm is one thing, but when it becomes the only option to get ashore or back afloat, it is a completely different matter, especially if there is any swell running.

You will need a long towline and a knife, should it all go wrong and there is a need to cut the rope free.

Find the most suitable place to land. Look for areas that have dark-coloured water moving up and down the rocks (see *Reading the Water* chapter) rather than breaking waves.

Assuming you are using a waist-mounted tow system, attach the towline to a deck line close to the cockpit and exit the kayak leaving it the right way up. Secure the paddle and any other loose items. When you are in the water, move the towline from close to the cockpit to the end of the kayak and ensure it is free to run to its full length.

Push the kayak away from the rocks and start swimming. When you are close to the rock, turn your feet towards the rock to protect yourself; this is when the kayak needs to be watched continuously, in case you need to fend it off.

As you land, find a place with good footing and once you are completely secure, start pulling the kayak gently towards you with the towline. As it approaches the rock take extra care and ensure you grab onto the toggle or deck line. Pull the kayak up onto the rock without damaging it too much and make sure it is high enough to be out of reach of the biggest waves.

SWIM TO SHORE AND LAND:

Swim to shore and land.

Launching from this situation is something that should be done only when there is no other option. Move the kayak close to the water and clip the tow to the end as before. Making sure the line is not tangled and is at its fullest length, launch the kayak into the water and follow it when safe to do so. It will probably be necessary to continue pushing the kayak in front of you as you make your way away from the rock. When a suitable distance from the rock, transfer the tow from the front of the kayak to close to the cockpit. Self rescue by whatever method works when you are tired, then remove and re-stow the tow system.

SWIM FROM SHORE AND SELF RESCUE:

Swim from shore and self rescue.

If you have an assistant it is possible to have them connect their tow to the kayak as well. This allows a more controlled trajectory towards the rock. They can even pull you and your kayak into an area of safe water.

This is a method of last resort and the danger should not be underestimated. It should not be undertaken when there is any other option available as the chance of injury and damage to equipment is huge.

A tow-assisted swimming launch.

SWIM WITH THE PADDLE

If there is a possibility you will have to swim into a rock wall to get off the water, you need to have developed a technique that keeps the paddle with you. The best solution I have found is to stay in the sitting position, as if still in the kayak, and use the paddle as normal. A shorter stroke than would generally be used works well and with practice it is possible to go a reasonable distance in control using this method. An added benefit is that the feet will be towards the rock acting as a shock absorber before your body makes contact.

Paddling while in a sitting position in the water. Photo: Kate Duffus

Repairs.

Repairs

Many years ago, I was assessing a Senior Instructor Award and one of the candidates had developed a way to carry out a repair which he had tested previously and was keen to show to us examiners. The 'holed' kayak was removed from the water and dried. He had cut a patch from a plastic lemonade bottle, and then poured superglue over the area to be repaired. With a wiping motion, he pressed the patch onto the hull and then gave it another wipe to ensure it was stuck. This resulted in the candidate becoming firmly attached to his kayak. He had used too much superglue and on the first wipe, the excess had transferred to his hand, which was now stuck to the patch, which was stuck to the hull.

It took us quite a while to prise his hand from the kayak using a paddle blade. If this had happened in a more dynamic situation the outcome could have been serious. As it was, the biggest concern was how sore everyone's sides were from the amount of laughter. The patch stayed on for the rest of the day and the candidate passed the award.

Many things may have to be repaired while sea kayaking. I have first-hand experience of several from the following list: broken paddle, torn spraydeck, torn clothing, burst drysuit gasket, lost hatch, damaged skeg / rudder, broken deck lines, broken toggle attachment, pulled out deck fitting, holed cooking pot, broken tent pole, torn tent fabric ... even a broken kayak, the list seems almost endless. Most of these repairs are fairly straightforward but some may require improvisation.

Sooner or later, there will come a time when the beautiful craft you have cared for so well will connect with another kayak, a sharp rock or some other unmovable object. The noise and the speed you stop at will let you know that you are about to become a repairer.

What you will have to do will depend on many factors such as whether you are afloat or on land, whether the kayak is composite or roto-moulded, whether it is a crack or a hole and where the damage is located.

KAYAK REPAIRS AFLOAT

Going ashore to effect repairs is the best option. If this is not possible, the first thing that has to be done is to remove the kayak from the water in order that it can be assessed for damage. The best way to do this is for the rescuer to come alongside facing the opposite direction to the casualty. The rescuer holds onto the deck lines, as described in the rescue section and stabilises the kayak so as to allow the casualty to exit and move onto the front deck of the rescuer's kayak where they should sit up facing towards the rescuer with both legs in the water to provide additional stability. The casualty's kayak is then moved at right angles and pulled over the rescuer's kayak before being turned upside down. When the cockpits align, the end of the casualty's kayak will be in the water and act as a huge stabiliser. The casualty is now in a good position to help with the repair. Dry the area of the repair and around it as much as possible, a rag or cloth will work well enough and friction from a dry hand will further help. This is to allow whatever repair material is being used to adhere to the hull.

Repair progression.

If it is raining, rig a shelter over the upturned hull using a storm cag or bivi shelter draped between the paddlers' heads; this will allow a better repair to be carried out.

After the repair is complete, reverse the procedure to get the casualty back into their kayak.

TEMPORARY REPAIRS

To effect temporary repairs, I have found the following materials very useful. The *Equipment* chapter goes into more detail about the suggested contents of a repair kit.

SURF WAX

Surf wax can be used to make a good malleable temporary repair by simply pressing it into the hole or crack and moulding both sides to conform to the hull shape. I used it to repair the bow of a roto-moulded kayak, the tip of which was taken off during a rock gardening session. The repair lasted four years until I carried out a permanent welded repair.

Surf wax repair.

DUCT TAPE

Duct tape will only work if the area is completely dry. The best option, if possible, is to wrap the tape all the way around the kayak so that it sticks to itself. Forget having a short length of tape rolled onto a pencil, a full roll is what is needed.

Duct tape wrap.

CLING FILM

Cling film or pallet wrap works well when it is wrapped completely around the kayak. Pallet wrap is best as it can, and should be, stretched before applying. As the tension comes off, the wrap consolidates almost into a sheet of plastic.

Pallet wrap.

PLUMBERS' (DENSO) TAPE

Plumbers' (Denso) tape is a very messy material to work with, and is best used as a pre-prepared patch stuck to a more rigid backing material in order to give strength to a hole.

Denso tape.

Pack the patch in a bag along with some gloves of the type that you get at a filling station and a cloth. This way it is a stand-alone repair patch system that will allow you to hold your paddle afterwards without it becoming covered with the goo that makes the tape stick so well.

FLASHBAND

Flashband is a less messy option than the Denso tape patch above but, for good adhesion, it requires the hull to be absolutely dry. Apply to the damaged area and rub with your hand to ensure the adhesive is warmed and spreads out below the patch, sticking to all the scratches on the kayak.

Flashband.

PLASTIC SHEET

This can be either a piece of plastic cut from a soft drinks bottle or a sheet of thick gauge polythene as used in the building trade. It is useful when the hole is quite large and the other repair materials need supporting.

Plastic sheet.

SKEGS

A jammed skeg is often caused by a small stone that has become wedged in the skeg box as you launch. Usually you can get a fellow paddler to extract the stone while you lean across somebody's deck for support.

Another common problem is that the wires that control skegs become kinked. If you use this type of skeg, you should carry a spare wire. However, these can only be replaced ashore. A temporary solution afloat is to get another paddler to push it back into the up position and fix it there with tape or cord. Without a skeg it may well be hard work, but you should be able to point in any direction. With the skeg jammed down you can only go in one.

PERMANENT REPAIRS

Permanent repairs can only be done ashore with some fairly specialised equipment, knowledge and skills. However, I have carried and used resin, hardener and glass cloth while on expedition in Greenland.

Welding a roto-moulded kayak is a tricky job requiring specialised tools and someone with experience of carrying out repairs of this type. A small blowtorch can be used and if a plastic of lower melting point is applied a repair can be made, but the application of surf wax is every bit as effective.

REPAIRS TO CLOTHING AND OTHER MATERIALS

Obviously for some items it is simpler to carry a spare, but there will come a time when something will happen which will need a different approach. This is when a good imagination and the ability to adapt is of benefit.

For fabrics, simply sew the parts together, and if the repair needs to be waterproof then apply either duct tape or surf wax as this will help keep the water out. Applying duct tape to both sides of a torn garment makes an effective repair. Rub both sides vigorously between your hands as this allows the adhesive to soften and permeate the fabric slightly and stick to the adhesive on the other piece of tape.

Duct tape can even be used to temporarily repair a split drysuit gasket. Use a single piece of duct tape to tape over the inside and outside of the gasket. The taped part of the gasket will obviously not stretch but there is enough elasticity in the non-taped part to allow you to pull a neck seal over your head, and it keeps the water out.

LOST OR DAMAGED HATCH COVER

Forget the old idea of carrying a sheet of polythene and a length of bungee to replace a hatch cover. It may work on land or in flat calm conditions, but it most definitely doesn't when the kayaks are heaving about in a confused sea. A much better idea is to have a set of emergency hatch covers made up and ready. These covers are made from a waterproof material and are adjustable to fit a number of hatch sizes. I carry three different sizes and they fit into one of the very smallest dry bags.

Emergency hatch cover.

Emergency hatch cover in use.

At a push it would be possible to wrap duct tape around the kayak and hatch opening but this would take quite some time and there would probably be quite a lot of water remaining in the compartment. Pallet wrap or cling film would work too.

Helicopter.
Photo: Donald MacPherson.

Rescue by Outside Agencies

As a birthday treat, I planned to paddle from Armadale to Camuscross on the Isle of Skye. The forecast was for southerly Force 9 or forty knots. It was definitely blowing this hard and probably gusting more, which meant that I was in for a good downwind run when I got clear of the big headland to the east of Knock Bay. There was no one else out on the water as it was early January. Morag dropped me off and then headed to a friend's house for coffee. I launched and paddled in the lee of the land until I reached the corner where the wind was hammering past, I then paddled at right angles to the wind to gain enough sea room to pass the headland four miles downwind.

It – was – exhilarating.

Three to four metre waves breaking at the top, I was surfing, bracing and smiling – lots. At one point, just as I cleared the headland, I thought I heard the deep sound of an engine but could see nothing so continued away from the road. I arrived in the bay after another 30 minutes of fun, put the kayak under some trees for shelter and then walked to the house.

When I got there I decided to use the hose to wash the salt off everything. As I was doing this, my mobile phone started ringing in my pocket. It was a neighbour, Pete, who ran an eco-tour company in Armadale using RIBs. He asked if I was out kayaking and when I said that I was home he told me that the Mallaig lifeboat was in Knock Bay.

I took off my drysuit, went into the house and called Stornoway Coastguard to let them know I was safe. After they had confirmed that I was the sea kayaker they were looking for and that there was no one else out on the water, they called off the search. They also said that they would tell the helicopter to return to base. I went outside to finish sorting my kit and the helicopter turned over the house and headed back to Stornoway.

Someone had seen me as I paddled past their house and when they looked again, had seen what they thought was a head in the water and did the correct thing by calling the coastguard. The engine noise I had heard was the lifeboat. I spoke with the lifeboat coxswain and the helicopter pilot later, and they both said that they didn't often get to practise in winds of that strength when there was no physical rescue to be done.

What a fantastic rescue service we have!

Sea kayakers are a self-sufficient group and don't like the idea of having to call on the rescue services. This is a laudable sentiment; no one cares to see the situation that has occured on land, where ill-prepared people call the rescue services because they are tired and want a lift down from the mountain or because they are 'feeling overwhelmed by their location', replicated on the sea. However, if something is starting to go wrong, or has gone wrong – **make the call, and make it early**.

The professional rescue services want to be called out before things go so far wrong that they have to pick up a body. They are also very happy to be called out early and stood down if they are not needed.

INITIAL DISTRESS ALERT OR CALLING FOR HELP

The coastguard service talks about the 'initial distress alert'. This can be made by someone involved in the incident or by someone outside, such as a concerned member of the public who has seen something out of the norm. It can take many forms; a mobile phone or VHF call, the activation of an EPIRB or PLB or the setting off of flares.

When making the call, it is worth remembering that the topography of the land around can sometimes limit the effectiveness of the communication. Below a moderately high cliff, there could be no phone or VHF radio signal, but half a mile offshore the signal might be fantastic.

MOBILE PHONE

Almost everyone has one of these. Enter the local coast-guard's phone number in your contact list, it can be found in the telephone directory, almanac or online. Make sure your phone is charged before setting out and in a water-proof case so that it doesn't get wet and can be operated while on the water.

Dialling 999 or 112 in the UK will get you through to the emergency services who will ask which service you

A selection of mobile phones.

Even when you appear to have no signal or are in an area of poor coverage, the networks prioritise emergency calls and use whichever network is available to connect your call. Mobile phone network providers are able to pinpoint the position of the transmission from your phone, which enables the rescue services to locate you more easily.

require – ask for the coastguard. They will ask you questions to gather the information they require to effect a successful rescue.

When you call 999, the assumption is that it is an emergency so you won't need to say **MAYDAY**.

VHF RADIO

As a responsible sea kayaker, you should have a VHF radio. Ideally it is attached to you and always switched on. This can be problematic if you are out for several days without an opportunity to recharge the battery.

One option is to have a set which will accept AA batteries in addition to the built-in rechargeable. Another is to switch the radio on when receiving weather forecasts and keep it off for the rest of the time. Obviously, this means that if you do have to call for help, there is the added time loss of switching the set on, but with the benefit of knowing that there is life in the battery.

A typical VHF radio.
Photo: Stephen Foley

You should have an operator's licence; in the UK this is issued by OFCOM and is free. You may wish to consider a certificate of competence in addition to the licence. Courses are generally run by sailing schools, and they teach and test best radio protocol.

The main benefit of using a VHF is that it achieves **two-way** communication. This allows:

◎ the casualty to make the emergency call,

◎ the casualty to speak to another human which can help reduce the stress,

◎ the casualty can let the rescue services know the nature of the problem so that they can respond more appropriately,

◎ the rescue services can keep you informed so that you know that rescue is on its way.

RADIO PROTOCOL TO BE USED IN AN EMERGENCY

PAN-PAN is an urgency signal, which is used to preface a VHF transmission when there is no immediate threat to a person's life. It means urgent assistance is needed and will trigger a rescue with reasonable urgency.

A PAN-PAN call can be escalated into a **MAYDAY** transmission. This generally means that there is an imminent threat to life and the rescue will reflect this heightened level of risk.

The decision when to use **MAYDAY** or **PAN-PAN** hinges on whether there is an imminent threat to life.

MAYDAY – Imminent threat to life.

PAN-PAN – Urgent assistance is required.

To make the call, ensure the set is switched on, set to full power and on channel 16.

Take a moment to compose yourself and then press the transmit button.

Speak slowly and clearly:

> **"MAYDAY, MAYDAY, MAYDAY"**
>
> **"THIS IS** (your call sign repeated three times)**"**
>
> **"MAYDAY** (your call sign)**"**
>
> **"MY POSITION IS** (latitude and longitude or true bearing and distance from a known object, or a description of your location as best as you can)**"**
>
> **"Nature of distress** (e.g. unconscious paddler, missing kayaker)**"**
>
> **"REQUIRE IMMEDIATE ASSISTANCE"**
>
> **"(Total number of) PEOPLE INVOLVED"**
>
> **"OVER"**

Release the transmit button and listen for an acknowledgement; if no acknowledgement is heard, repeat the mayday until there is a response.

The coastguard personnel are trained in speaking to individuals who are in a stressful situation. They will do everything they can to make the conversation easy. They need to ensure they have all the appropriate information before committing their assets. You will not get into trouble if you do not use the correct protocol, it just makes the coastguard radio operator's job easier.

PLB

When activated, a Personal Locator Beacon (PLB) sends a unique identifier to the Cospas-Sarsat satellite system which can pinpoint the location to within a few metres, typically within five minutes, though it can take up to forty-five minutes depending on the satellite coverage. The information is then relayed to the closest coastguard station and they set about coordinating the rescue.

Most units have a secondary homing transmitter, which allows the rescue services to home in on your position once they are in the general area. Additionally, most have a flashing SOS light, which can also be used to attract attention. The lithium power source contained allows a shelf life of approximately six years, and a minimum of twenty-four hours continuous operation once activated.

DIGITAL SELECTIVE CALLING

DSC (Digital Selective Calling) on a VHF radio set is not the same as a PLB. The DSC range is just slightly more than that of a VHF, as the same infrastructure of antennae is utilised. The digital signal produced by the DSC set travels slightly further than voice modulation and can pinpoint the position of the transmitter by using GPS, as long as the set is within communicating distance from the coastguard aerial, or that of another water user.

The PLB set must be registered with the relevant national authority, and in the UK can be used on land as well as on the water. The registration is very useful as it gives the coast-guard valuable information, for example, allowing them to determine whether the casualty is a kayaker or a large yacht.

A downside to PLBs is that there is no way of knowing that the distress signal has been picked up or that help is on its way to your location. The set will need to be held as directed in the user instructions with the aerial pointing to the sky until help arrives.

If accidentally activated, or if the situation you were in decreases in danger before the rescue services arrive on the scene, switch the unit off and contact the relevant rescue services as soon as possible.

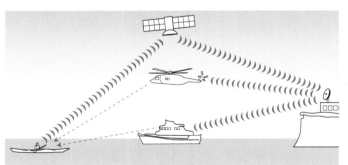

Kayaker activates PLB distress alert. Signal is relayed via satellite to the Maritime and Coastguard Agency (MCA). The MCA tasks assets to attend.

EPIRB

An EPIRB (Emergency Position-indicating Radio Beacon) is large and floats and is more suitable for larger vessels. It is essentially the same as a PLB (which is more practical for sea kayakers) in terms of how it alerts the rescue services.

FLARES

For a flare to be effective as the 'initial distress alert', someone has to see it, know what it is and inform the coastguard. This is a major downside to flares, as is their short shelf life. As the casualty, you have no way of telling if the flare has been seen or the rescue services alerted. Flares do work well, however, once the rescue services are in sight, to help them pinpoint your position.

To set off a parachute flare, it is best to lean across the deck of another kayak with your hands over the side, close to the water. The safety and use of flares is discussed in more detail in the next chapter.

Smoke, pinpoint and parachute flares.

WHAT HAPPENS NEXT?

When the coastguard has been informed of the need for a rescue, they will notify the closest 'asset', this is a lifeboat or helicopter not involved in another incident. As a general guide the search and rescue helicopters around the UK are in the air within 15 minutes of the distress call during the day, and 45 minutes at night. Lifeboats normally take around 10 minutes from the initial call to launch.

The coastguard will continue to communicate with the caller if the distress alert was made through a VHF radio or phone.

Lifeboat. Photo: Donald MacPherson

SARIS

The Search and Rescue Information System (SARIS) is an integrated search and rescue planning tool. It allows rescue agencies to work out the most likely position of the casualty and therefore the most appropriate search area and pattern of search.

The search area is determined by many factors including the prevailing meteorological and oceanographic conditions, the type of vessel being looked for (a sailing boat will drift much faster than a person in the water) and the 'target trajectory'.

In the coastguard office, a PLB activation will show on the screen and the operator will input information such as 'type of craft'. An appropriate search pattern will emerge. It is also possible for the operator to manually input a position when given by a member of the public or when the initial distress alert is made by VHF radio.

The information is then relayed to the rescue service most suited to the task and the search pattern can be optimised for a water or air-based search.

Coastguard officer operating SARIS.
Photo: Stephen Foley

ATTRACTING ATTENTION

Anything that is out of the ordinary will attract the attention of the lifeboat or helicopter crews.

STROBE

A simple strobe light, mounted high on the shoulder will attract attention from as far as two miles during the day and many more at night. A light flashing above the water will be much more likely to be seen – when submerged it will produce more of a glow than a flash.

FLARE

A red pinpoint flare will enable the rescue services to determine the location of the casualty and wind direction better than an orange smoke flare. This is because in strong winds, the smoke from the orange smoke flare is dispersed and flattened on the sea, making it harder to see.

The very hot flame of the red pinpoint flare can be picked up by infrared cameras if used by the rescue crews and the smoke produced is hot and rises, so can be seen from further away. A standard-size pinpoint flare will burn for around 60 seconds while a day / night pinpoint and smoke combined will last around 12 seconds.

VHF RADIO

Both the lifeboat and helicopter are equipped with VHF homing devices. These lock onto the signal produced when transmitting. Often the crew will instruct a slow count to ten and down again to enable a good position fix.

LASER FLARE

These compact rescue flares produce a beam of light which, when moved across a target, is seen as a flash. They are very effective day or night and the replaceable lithium battery ensures they have a good life span.

FLASHLIGHT

Any light, the brighter the better, easy to direct towards the approaching rescuers is good. It is best if it is waterproof.

LIFEBOAT

When alerted of an incident the coastguard sets off the crew pagers. Shortly afterwards, the crew members arrive, get changed and ready the boat to launch. Once the crew have assembled, they are briefed as to the type of incident, number of casualties and location.

Inshore lifeboats can usually be launched quicker than the all-weather boats as the latter are not always afloat.

Lifeboats are equipped with direction-finding equipment, similar to that found on helicopters. It usually requires the casualty to transmit on a slow count for best effect.

Direction-finding ping on lifeboat. Photo: Mark Gray

As the search area is approached, the crew will all be on watch. They will use search-lights and night vision goggles if appropriate. The biggest problem when trying to locate a kayak is that it is such a small target. Even in a small chop, kayaks can become hidden between the waves. This is why it is important, if you are paddling with others, to keep together as a group.

Kayakers mostly choose to hug the coastline. A big lifeboat will not venture into shallow water but may launch the smaller 'daughter' boat, an inflatable more suited to working close to shore operated by two crew members who remain in contact with the main lifeboat. This small boat can make a detailed search and is able to act as a shuttle for casualties as required.

As with any rescue, the crew will not really know what they are going to have to do until they arrive on the scene and assess the complete situation. If the casualty has been in the water for any length of time, the norm is to use a double sling lift to keep the body in a near-horizontal position. This is to reduce the chance of hydrostatic or post-rescue collapse (see *Cold Water Immersion* chapter). Another recovery tool is the rescue scramble net which is lowered over the side of the lifeboat. Any casualty, who is able to, can then climb to the safety of the lifeboat.

The main function of the lifeboat is to save lives at sea. Equipment is secondary and it is up to the individual coxswain as to whether the kayaks will be taken on board or not.

HELICOPTER

The helicopter is always primed and ready to fly. When the call comes through to the helicopter base, some of the crew will begin changing into their immersion equipment. The captain will make decisions about whether extra fuel will be needed and how long it will take to arrive on the scene.

A rescue carried out during the day is much easier than at night, when the workload of the crew increases dramatically. Most of the work at night is about keeping the aircraft safe and therefore the crew has less capacity to do the searching. Searchlights or infrared cameras are used, but nothing is as good as eyes in daylight.

Before the helicopter arrives on site ensure all loose items are secured, either by putting them into hatches, or tying them to deck lines.

It is easiest for the crew to lift a casualty from land or from the deck of a boat. If you are on land, place all the kayaks together with any loose items secured, and have one member of the group lie across them to stop them blowing about. If on the water, have the casualty lie across the front of the kayaks with their head off to one side.

As the helicopter approaches, never assume it knows where you are, keep signalling until it is obvious that the crew have seen you.

A helicopter is noisy and can be distracting and disorienting. Make sure that everyone knows what is about to happen because once the helicopter is overhead, communicating will be all but impossible.

Normally, the helicopter will position downwind of the casualty and the winchman will be lowered until he is around two to three metres above the surface of the water. A helicopter in flight acquires an electrostatic charge and this has to be discharged before any contact is made. The static discharge line will hang below the winchman and, as it touches the water, will earth the aircraft rendering it static free. Only once this has been done, will it be safe to touch the line or the winchman.

The pilot will manoeuvre towards the casualty. As they do this, the helicopter will rise to reduce the effect of the downdraft on the surface of the water. A technique called 'trawling', where the winchman's legs are in the water, is used as this gives him some form of directional control. The winchman will aim to arrive near the head of the casualty but the rotor wash from the helicopter may blow the raft off course. If this happens the winchman will make contact with the raft and move to the best position. He will be unable to communicate easily so let him position the strop under the arms of the casualty.

After the casualty has been removed from the raft, the helicopter will move away keeping the winchman and casualty just a few feet above the surface of the water. The helicopter will start descending as the winchman and casualty are recovered into the helicopter. At no point will they be more than 15 metres above the water. This is to prevent possible injury if they were accidentally dropped.

Throughout the winching process, it is important that the raft is held together firmly. A breakup of the raft could endanger everyone involved.

ADVICE FROM THE PROFESSIONALS

Retro-reflective tape – Most sea kayaking clothing has reflective piping sewn on but kayaks and paddles do not come with this as standard. You can purchase retro-reflective tape from any ship chandler or online. Adorn your kayak and paddles with a few strips, round off the corners so that it sticks better. Even a minimum amount of tape applied to your gear is enough to allow you to be located.

Hand warmers – Consider carrying a hand warmer. If your hands are so cold that they can't operate a VHF radio or PLB, then you won't be able to make the initial distress alert, never mind any of the follow-up communication.

Red pinpoint flares are better than smoke – The light from red pinpoint flares is much more visible from the air and through infrared cameras and night vision goggles. The smoke is hot and rises from the flare. It isn't flattened on the sea as is the smoke from the orange smoke flare.

Laser flare – The laser flare gives off a bright fan of light that is so conspicuous that it requires investigating. It can be seen for many miles day or night.

PLB then VHF radio then flare – Use a PLB to initiate the initial distress alert, this gives the coastguard a good position fix, along with details of who has set off the unit. Follow this up with a call on the VHF radio and finally, once the rescue team is in sight, with a red pinpoint flare to give an exact location and important wind direction information.

Let them do what they need to do – They have trained for many years and know the best ways to deal with most incidents. The crews may appear to be gruff and uncaring, but they are only being efficient. Your rescue may be one of many that they have been involved in during their watch.

Finally, if you ever need their help I suggest you thank them – as best as you know how. The lifeboat crews are, for the most part, volunteers with normal jobs. The helicopter crews are employed full-time to fulfil search and rescue duties, but they still appreciate a thank you.

Coloured water.

Flare.

Flares

I have set off many different types of flare over a number of years. Always while warm and standing on dry land. On land this is all well and good, but when filming for the *Emergency Situations* film on DVD 3 in the series *Sea Kayak with Gordon Brown*, several things happened that made me rethink how I would use a flare when afloat in a kayak.

We had anchored deep in a loch on the west side of Harris on the Outer Hebrides, then arranged with the coastguard to set off a parachute flare, followed by a pinpoint. We had already received permission to do this. The time of 22.30 was decided upon, as it would be dark enough to see the effect of the flare, but still light enough to have general illumination for the shot. Another yacht had anchored within 100 metres of our position.

I changed and thought through my actions and script as I got ready to go on the water. For a bit of a laugh, I decided to wind Simon up. As he was preparing the cameras and sound recording equipment, I borrowed leather welding gauntlets and safety glasses from the skipper of the boat. I put these on along with my helmet and waited for a reaction. It was priceless. Simon asked, through a barrage of interesting language, how we would reconcile my outfit with me never wearing a helmet for any of the other filming. Everyone else on the boat was watching, and we all had a good laugh about the silliness of wearing all that protective equipment.

I removed all the extra protection, launched from the tender and with the cameras running, talked about how to set off a flare, then I proceeded to fire the parachute. I was holding onto the tube firmly with both hands as I pulled the trigger. At the time, I had no idea what happened next as the flare ignited and took off. The first thing I remember is picking the tube out of the water and thinking that my hand was a bit sore.

It transpired that the recoil from the ignition and launch was so violent that the tube was forced through my hands and onto the spraydeck. After hitting the deck, it bounced upwards and landed in the water next to me. Reviewing the footage from the deck-mounted camera, the four images below show the trajectory of the tube. Each image is taken at 1/25th of a second interval. It was no wonder that my hand was sore, it was bruised and I was lucky not to have been burned. The incident did get me thinking though, and I wished that I had kept all the protective gear on.

Parachute flare firing sequence. Photo: Simon Willis

When holding onto the pinpoint, I was very concerned that the heat and sparks would end up burning my cag. It was then that I realised that by changing my grip very slightly, I could minimise the risk of damaging my equipment.

Throughout the whole episode, which lasted about forty minutes, not one person from the yacht anchored about 100 metres away ever looked outside to see what the noise was about.

In the *Rescue by Outside Agencies* chapter, I have already touched on flares and pyrotechnics. Here we will explore the subject in greater depth.

GENERAL SAFETY INFORMATION

Keep the flares as dry as possible but always available in case they are needed. A sturdy dry bag attached to the deck lines is as good as any other method. It is not good enough to have a sealed pack of flares inside the kayak, or behind the skeg box, because although you want to keep them dry, they need to be accessible at all times.

Drybag with flares.

On deck there is also a greater chance that you will rinse and look after them, rather than if they are kept in another type of container, possibly hidden from view.

When using a smoke flare, hold it on your downwind side and remember that whatever the smoke gets onto will become orange too.

When igniting a pinpoint flare, wear gloves, if possible, as the heat generated by the burning magnesium is significant. Again, keep it on the downwind side and instead of holding the flare upright and vertical, hold it upside down and vertical. This ensures that the burning materials drop off into the water, rather than onto you and your clothing. The difference is only a few centimetres in height and as you will be able to see your rescuer, there is no significant benefit to be gained by holding it high.

Be prepared for the dark and cold when the flare has completed its burn. Due to the intensity of the light produced, there will be a considerable period of night vision loss, which will cause disorientation and possibly seasickness. This would add to the difficulties of the rescue. Even if you look towards the flare with your eyes closed, the brightness is such that it will leave an image on the retina for some time. The flare burns very hot and the air temperature will feel cold as soon as it has finished burning. The outer steel casing, however, will be glowing red hot so take care not to burn anything. Dipping the used flare in the water is a good way of rendering it safe, although in a real rescue situation I can't imagine anyone keeping hold of the spent flare tube; it is much more likely to be dropped into the water.

Flare inverted.

To deploy a parachute flare from your kayak, lie face down over the back of another kayak. This keeps your face protected and will ensure that the tube, if it proves to be uncontrollable as in the story above, ends up in the water. If in the water, lie across the back deck of your own kayak and fire from this position.

Firing position when you are on your own.

Firing position when using a parachute flare, lying over another kayak.

TRADITIONAL 'PYROTECHNIC' FLARES

Pyrotechnic flares all produce a very bright light or smoke, involve potentially explosive substances, burn very hot, and need careful storage and handling.

DAY / NIGHT FLARE

The day / night flare is two flares in one. The 'day' part is a smoke flare that lasts around twelve seconds and the 'night' part is a red pinpoint, which lasts about eight seconds, which is not very long. These are good for keeping close at hand, in a buoyancy aid pocket. Although fitted with an O ring to stop water from entering the firing mechanism, it is worthwhile wrapping a piece of electrical tape around the join to further ensure waterproofness. If you do this, leave the end of the tape doubled back on itself so that it can be removed easily when required, especially if you are wearing gloves.

Day / night flare.   *Extra tape with release tab.*

PINPOINT

Pinpoint flares cannot be used to initiate an emergency call, but they are invaluable for guiding rescuers to your position. Pinpoint flares make little noise until fully ignited but then they burn with a spluttering fierceness that threatens to set fire to everything close by. They produce a bright red light, lots of heat and a bit of smoke. The pinpoint flare is the preferred option if a helicopter is approaching as the hot smoke lifts from the water and gives the pilot a good indication of the surface wind speed and direction.

Pinpoint flare. Photo: Simon Willis

SMOKE FLARE

Like the pinpoint flare, the smoke flare is a means of guiding rescuers to your position and cannot be used as an initial call for help. Smoke flares splutter into action then emit a cloud of dense orange smoke. If a reasonable wind is blowing, the smoke flattens on the water and follows the wind eddies created in the lee of the waves. In a

Smoke flare. Photo: Simon Willis

more gentle wind, the smoke rises and spreads downwind in a large plume. This may be a good option when surface craft are attempting to locate your position. Just be aware, though, that everything will end up covered in nasty orange dust, which is almost impossible to clean off.

PARACHUTE FLARE

Parachute flares go off with a 'WHOOSH' and, as the story at the start of the chapter illustrates, quite a bit of recoil. They then bang some 300 metres into the air before igniting and dropping a burning red light suspended on a parachute. The parachute flare is a suitable means of attracting attention in the initial phases of a rescue. There are drawbacks to using them of course:

Parachute flare fired from a kayak. Photo: Mark Gray

- ◎ your hands have to be working well enough to manipulate the flare, operate the firing mechanism and hold onto it as it burns,

- ◎ where there are high cliffs or low clouds, the deployed flare will be ineffective as it will be below the top of the cliffs, or in the cloud, and nobody will be able to see it.

When setting off a parachute flare, aim it slightly into the wind. When the flare has completely burned out, set off another one straight away, as this confirms to someone who thinks they have seen a distress flare that it is actually what they saw. The bang is loud enough to attract someone's attention.

The major downside to all flares, is that someone has to be looking in your direction in order to see the light. If unseen, help will not be on its way.

NEW TECHNOLOGY FLARES

A number of companies are developing alternatives to pyrotechnic flares. These don't have any burning parts and don't go out of date every three years or so. At the time of writing, the authorities are not accepting new technology flares instead of pyrotechnic flares on vessels for which carrying flares is mandatory.

My advice, repeated by the coastguard, the lifeboat and SAR helicopter crews, is that whatever type of flare you choose to carry, always have a red pinpoint flare as well. This is invaluable to the rescue crews, as it gives an indication of wind strength and direction when deployed, as well as plenty of heat that can be picked up with the thermal imaging cameras carried on board the rescue craft.

LASER FLARES

Laser flares are small waterproof handheld lights, fantastic for fixing a position when help is on its way. Most are powered by lithium batteries, which are user-replaceable and should last for many years if unused. If used continuously, the light lasts around eight hours.

The beam is eye-safe at a distance of more than four metres and can be seen from 50 kilometres away. A fan of light is produced which spreads as the distance from the source increases. A prospective rescuer will see a brief, but bright, flash as the 'fan' crosses their vision. At 20 kilometres, the width of the fan is around 2000 metres long making it easy to target at a rescuer. It is also a great device for locating other group members or lost equipment, as long as there is some retro-reflective tape attached.

Using a hand as a sight for a laser flare.

To use, simply turn it on and point the end that emits the light towards the target. To aim, make a 'sight' with the thumb and index finger of your other hand, at arm's length from the laser. This is useful because you will not be able to see where the light falls, especially in the case of an aircraft which could be many miles away.

I keep my rescue laser flare attached inside my buoyancy aid at all times. It is worth noting that this type of flare is suitable to take aboard a flight if you ever choose to fly to a distant paddling destination.

LED FLARE

This 'flare' contains a very bright set of LEDs that flash in a similar manner to a magnesium flare. The solid light is periodically interrupted and replaced by a flashing S-O-S in Morse code. This safe, reusable unit is powered by lithium batteries, the light output lasts for around six hours and is visible for about three miles at sea level. It is a suitable means of attracting attention after the initial distress alert has been made.

LED flare. Photo: Kate Duffus

Waiting for rescue.

Cold Water Immersion

Hugh, a friend, planned a paddle from my house in Breakish to pass the villages of Kyle of Lochalsh and Kyleakin, through the tide race at Kyle Rhea, to the Isle Ornsay Hotel, where he would be met by his wife. The weather was suitable for this trip and when Hugh set off, the wind was light, Force 2–3 and from the west. This meant that he would have assistance for the first part of the journey and then shelter as he went further south through Kyle Rhea and towards Isle Ornsay. All went well, and as he was ahead of his planned timings, he made a short lunch stop just south of the village of Kylerhea.

Hugh got back on the water and set off southwards. Upon reaching the corner, he came across an area of very rough water; the wind had backed more southerly. He capsized, failed a roll and wet exited. He attempted several self rescues, which were unsuccessful due to the sea state. A local fishing boat came alongside and suggested they take him back to Kyleakin but instead, Hugh asked them to tow him closer to the shore so that he could complete his journey to meet his wife.

Due to the shallow water in the bay, the boat could not get very close to the shore, so at some point Hugh said that he was fine and could easily swim the last part with his kayak and paddle. The fishing boat left.

Hugh became tangled in the weed in the bay. He was spotted by someone in the RSPB hide, some way off, up the hill. This person made a phone call to Alan, a local, who changed into a wetsuit and made his way to where Hugh was. Wading into the water, Alan could not quite reach Hugh and at this point Hugh stopped functioning. Alan swam the remaining metres, and pulled Hugh back to shore before collecting the kayak and paddle.

Overcome with both exhaustion and hypothermia, Hugh was 'in the dead zone' according to the paramedic who attended the scene. The first that Hugh knew of the situation was when he came to, surrounded by people and with a helicopter nearby. He was loaded into the helicopter, taken to hospital, and later released to be collected by his wife several hours later than planned.

Hugh later told me that he was not aware of becoming hypothermic (he had previous experience of this condition), or even cold. He was suitably dressed for the time of year, the conditions and the possibility of being in the water. I met Alan some time after the event and he told me that he was in two minds whether to go into the water or not, but he was glad that he had made the right choice on the day.

The inability of the human body to withstand extremes of temperature is well known, but cold is the one which concerns us most. Our body loses heat in still water some 25 times faster than in air of the same temperature, and in flowing water around 32 times faster. By selecting appropriate clothing for the activity, the consequences of immersion are reduced – but not eliminated.

COLD WATER IMMERSION RESPONSE

After being immersed in cold water, breathing patterns change for the first minute.

First there is an involuntary, automatic gasp reflex, due to the rapid cooling of the skin. If the head is under the water at this stage, drowning occurs, as water is drawn into the lungs, instead of air. Fortunately as sea kayakers we are likely to be more inured to this, as we are always close to the water and are often splashed in the face.

Hyperventilation is the next reflex. This deep, rapid breathing causes a decrease in carbon dioxide in the blood which makes us feel light-headed and short of breath, and causes the heart to beat more rapidly. The physiological effect of hyperventilation will diminish, however anxiety can cause prolonged psychological hyperventilation, which can lead to fainting. Controlling breathing is a major step in avoiding hyperventilation.

Peripheral vasoconstriction also occurs – the blood flow to the surface of the skin and limbs is reduced to allow the core to keep the warmer blood. The heart will work harder to keep the same volume of blood circulating and as a result, blood pressure will rise. If the casualty has an underlying heart condition, either known or previously unknown, this stress can cause cardiac arrest. Upon removal from cold water, this vasoconstriction stops quite quickly and things settle down.

Incapacitation due to the cold normally happens after between five to fifteen minutes of immersion. The vasoconstriction which protected the core by keeping it warm, now causes the nerves and muscles on the periphery to stop functioning. This is a critical time as coordinated movement is compromised, first in the hands and feet and shortly after in the arms and legs. The ability to hold onto items of equipment is vital and when fine motor control is lost in the hands everything becomes much harder to accomplish.

Have you ever tried to light a match while wearing boxing gloves? Now think about using your VHF radio, or operating a flare. When the legs and arms stop functioning properly you will be unable to keep your head above the surface of the water unless wearing a flotation device of some description.

HYPOTHERMIA

The time that it takes to become hypothermic varies from person to person and with water temperature. One thing worth mentioning is that it takes between 20 and 40 minutes for a normal, healthy adult to become hypothermic in water at 2°C. This is a vital piece of information, as most people think that hypothermia occurs quickly and they panic as a result. There is generally enough time to make good, considered decisions, and carry out the necessary actions that could save your life. (Although the waters around the United Kingdom never become as cold as 2°C, all of the research carried out into hypothermia is done with water at this temperature).

Hypothermia is considered to have three distinct phases (mild, moderate and severe). The table below shows the development of hypothermia, starting with a 'normal' core temperature of 37°C, from entry into water at 2°C wearing normal clothing.

PHASE OF HYPOTHERMIA	TIME IN WATER	CORE TEMPERATURE	CHARACTERISTICS
Mild	Up to 30 minutes	35–32°C	Shivering
Moderate	30–90 minutes	32–28°C	Shivering stops
Severe	90–180 minutes	Less than 28°C	Cooling continues until cardiac arrest

Core temperature is not easily measured while on the water so a more general set of indicators must be used.

MILD HYPOTHERMIA

Mild hypothermia (35–32°C) symptoms are not always obvious but can include:

◎ constant shivering

◎ tiredness

◎ low energy

◎ cold or pale skin

◎ hyperventilation

If a casualty can consciously stop their shivering they are at this stage.

MODERATE HYPOTHERMIA

Moderate hypothermia (32–28°C) symptoms include:

◎ inability to think or pay attention

◎ confusion

◎ loss of judgement or reasoning

◎ difficulty in moving around

◎ loss of coordination

◎ drowsiness

◎ slurred speech

◎ hypoventilation (slow, shallow breathing)

> These symptoms can also be thought of as the '-umbles' and are a good indication that someone is becoming a casualty:
>
> Mumbles
>
> Stumbles
>
> Fumbles
>
> Grumbles
>
> Tumbles

Other considerations

Unfortunately there are other medical conditions, which can cause similar symptoms; hypoglycaemia, diabetes and stroke are the main ones, not forgetting the effects of alcohol.

Normally when someone gets cold and is shivering to warm up, a serious indicator of the deterioration of their condition is when the shivering stops. This is because shivering is designed to keep our large muscles warm so that we are ready for action. If we are still cold and stop shivering, it means that our body has decided that it is more important to conserve heat in the core than to keep the large muscles warm. Emergency medical help is required immediately.

SEVERE HYPOTHERMIA

Severe hypothermia (less than 28°C) symptoms can include:

◎ unconsciousness

◎ shallow or no breathing

◎ weak, irregular pulse, or no pulse

◎ dilated pupils

When someone is suffering from severe hypothermia they may appear to be dead. In this case the casualty must be taken to hospital, as with correct medical treatment it may be possible to resuscitate them.

"A casualty is only dead when they are warm and dead ..."

COLLAPSE DURING RESCUE

When struggling to survive, the senses are heightened, adrenaline and other stress hormones flow through the body to assist survival.

At the point of rescue, mental relaxation often causes a decrease in the release of these hormones and it is very likely that the casualty collapses. Muscles stop working and in extreme cases, the blood pressure drops enough to lead to cardiac arrest.

POST-RESCUE COLLAPSE

The hydrostatic pressure exerted on the body when immersed in the water forces the blood to stay near the core and away from the extremities. When the body is removed from the water, this pressure ceases and as a result the warm blood from the core flows out again to the arms and especially the legs, causing a drop in blood pressure, which can be enough to stop the heart. Additionally, the cooler blood from the extremities circulates and cools the core further.

The rescue services are fully aware of this physiological process and have developed a system of recovery where the casualty is kept in a horizontal position when being lifted from the water. This is employed in every rescue of a casualty who is suspected of having been immersed in the water for any length of time.

A hydrostatic lift in progress. Photos: Mark Gray

AFTERDROP

This occurs after removal from the cold environment and is the persistent drop in core body temperature. This afterdrop can happen even when the casualty is only mildly hypothermic. The most satisfactory way to treat this is to remove any wet clothing, replace with dry, then provide decent insulation and shelter to protect against further heat loss. This is obviously only realistic once ashore. If possible, put the casualty in a group shelter with the rest of the group, the warm moist air will assist in the warming process.

A casualty wearing dry clothes, insulated from the ground and inside a group shelter with the other group members.

If getting off the water isn't an option, have the casualty raft up with at least one other group member and get them inside a group shelter while still sitting in their kayaks. Unfortunately, this may make them seasick.

Avoid giving caffeine or alcohol to the casualty, also do not rub their skin or apply direct heat to warm it up. All of this causes dilation of the blood vessels near the surface of the skin, which will lead to more complications and a worsening of hypothermia.

WATER TEMPERATURE

Water temperatures around the world vary between -2°C and 35°C according to data collected by the NASA Aqua satellite. This measurement is taken in the top 2mm of the surface of the water. Even in the warmest water, when we are immersed, our body temperature **will** drop because the water is cooler than our body temperature. Of course in the tropics, the rate of cooling will not be as fast as in cold water, but it will still happen.

EATING TO KEEP WARM

Having a nice cup of tea and some chocolate is a start, but there are better things to eat to keep warm. Anything that provides energy is good – sugar is good for a morale boost but not the best thing to supply energy over a long, cold day. A more satisfactory option is to eat muesli bars, they come wrapped and are fairly waterproof so can be kept in a buoyancy aid pocket. Mixed fruit and nuts are great although they are slightly more difficult to carry, requiring a small bag kept in a pocket (nuts by themselves can stand being immersed in salt water and won't taste too bad afterwards). If you are planning on being out for an extended length of time in very cold conditions, then anything with high fat content is excellent, small cheeses wrapped in wax are particularly good. For a quick sugar hit, any of the sports gels work well, but I have found that I then need to drink quite a lot as they coat the inside of my mouth.

HELP YOURSELF

As mentioned earlier, the body loses heat up to 32 times quicker in water than in the air. Maximise your chances of survival by removing as much of your body as possible from the water. If you cannot self rescue, just lying across the rear deck of your kayak will increase your survival time significantly.

Casualty lying across the rear deck of their kayak to minimise heat loss to the water.

After the initial shock of being immersed in cold water, there are some important things that you must do:

◎ the first is to put on a neoprene hood and gloves if these are accessible,

◎ then prepare the flares for firing and,

◎ activate the initial distress alert using your PLB and VHF radio.

Casualty wearing a neoprene hood and gloves and holding a PLB, with a flare close to hand.

Without gloves and a hood, you might become so cold that you are unable to fire a flare or operate your radio when the emergency services arrive on the scene.

BUDDY HELP

Use a buddy system to ensure that everyone within the paddling party has another person paying close attention to them, particularly when paddling in conditions where the cold could be an issue. With buddies looking out for each other, the telltale signs of hypothermia may be picked up much sooner. Keep the communications going and ensure everyone is eating and drinking enough of the right things frequently.

Cooling down.

Health Issues

So there I was minding my own business, connecting the muscles of your forearm to the bones of your right hand. I had done this for almost fifty years without you even knowing I was there, or even what I was. I was telling you to go easy on me, but you were not listening. That morning you decided to put me in a tight latex cuff, much too tight in my opinion and then your hand went into a thick neoprene glove. As you massaged your wrist, that was me telling you to slow down and not do so much. When you got into your kayak and held onto your paddle, it was nice and lightweight, but the diameter of the shaft was a bit on the big side for your small hands. It was your new paddle, it matched your kayak and you were going to use it no matter what. Your gloves made the shaft seem much larger and I was still trying to tell you to take care of me. As you set off with the rest of the group you gripped onto your paddle very tightly, not because you were afraid of dropping it, but more that you were on the edge of your comfort zone in those conditions. You knew I was complaining, as every time you had a chance, you would give me a quick rub and hope that I would be comforted.

By early afternoon I was screaming at you and you knew that I was not at all happy. When you came ashore and took all of your equipment off you looked at your arm and were surprised that there was a large lump, two finger widths above your wrist, where there had been some discomfort earlier. You put your ear against me and when you flexed your wrist, I growled. In fact I growled so loudly that you felt that everyone around you could hear me.

You asked some of the other group members what was wrong and immediately they knew, 'Paddler's wrist or tenosynovitis' was the consensus and they were correct. Plenty of rest they said. Change your paddle they said. Of course you didn't listen to them, you knew your body better than them and anyway, some anti-inflammatory tablets would help soothe me. How wrong you were. I kept you awake through the night, shouted at you as you ate breakfast, growled every time you made me work, screamed as you put all of your equipment on. I had to finally resort to burning you so that you would stop.

When you went home, you saw a specialist who immobilised me and ensured I was looked after better than I had been recently. It took weeks of care to stop me growling and five months to return to my normal size. I was glad, when you paddled again, that you had dealt with all the things that hurt me, and I know that now you will listen and take much better care of me.

This section covers a small selection of health issues. For a more complete look at health and preventative measures, I thoroughly recommend the *Oxford Handbook of Expedition Medicine*. Some of the problems discussed here are not of the immediate first aid trauma type, instead they relate to a gradual worsening of a condition that, if left untreated, will spoil your time on the water, sometimes for several months. I have suffered from them all, to a greater or lesser degree. For example, I currently have bony growths in both ears and am doing my best to stop them worsening by using the preventative measures listed below.

HEAT INJURIES

It's hard to imagine suffering from any sort of heat injuries when kayaking in a UK environment, but it can and does happen. The sun delivers a huge amount of energy to the earth and if we don't take measures to protect ourselves, it can injure us in a variety of ways.

SUNBURN

Sunburn is a problem in all regions of the earth, but more so when approaching the polar areas. The ozone layer in the atmosphere is thinner here, especially over Antarctica. Ozone filters out harmful ultraviolet radiation. The effect of a thinner ozone layer is that exposure to the sun's rays results in damage to unprotected body parts more quickly than you would expect. Hands are particularly vulnerable. A hat or cap with a brim or peak will help lessen the exposure – especially if, like me, your thatch is starting to thin.

Sunscreen applied liberally onto all exposed skin. Photo: Roger Aguirre Smith

A good quality sunscreen is a must, the higher the factor of protection, the better. Anything less than SPF 50 isn't really suitable to stop your skin burning. Apply before exposure and reapply at regular intervals, making sure that all exposed skin is covered.

UNDERSTANDING SPF RATINGS

If your skin starts to burn after 10 minutes of unprotected exposure to the sun, then SPF 15 reduces the amount of UV reaching your skin by a factor of 15. This means that it would take 15 times longer before your skin starts to burn than if you had none on, in this case 150 minutes or 2½ hours. Given that we are likely to be out paddling far longer than that, a higher SPF rating is advisable.

Hat with brim to minimise exposure to UV.

REFLECTED LIGHT SUNBURN

Reflected light sunburn is caused by exposure to UV rays bouncing off a highly reflective surface, such as water or snow. Vulnerable areas are those which are always facing the water, in particular below the ears, chin and nostrils. If unprotected, they will become badly burned. When applying sunscreen, pay special attention to these parts.

SNOW BLINDNESS

Snow blindness is caused by exposure to reflected UV light off snow, water or even concrete. It is very painful (it feels like someone has rubbed sand into your eyes) and prevention is much better than having to get treatment.

A peaked hat will reduce some of the effect of the reflected light by absorbing it. Wearing sunglasses is essential, but make sure that they are good quality and block UVA and UVB. My eyes are always very sore after a sunny day on the water.

Sunglasses.

I particularly struggle when it is not sunny but very bright. This is because a light cloud cover allows UV light through, and in addition, it reflects back to the ground a proportion of light that has bounced off the earth's surface, thus concentrating the UV rays.

The only field treatment for snow blindness is to rest in a dark place, use cold tea as an eyewash and apply cold compresses. There are eye drops available that will stop the pain. However, these should not be used to allow the casualty to continue paddling, as further exposure could cause serious eye damage.

HYPERTHERMIA

When the body overheats, it starts to malfunction and needs to be cooled. If paddling in warm conditions wearing a dry suit, it is possible to succumb to exertion hyperthermia. Even a breathable suit cannot transport the heat away from the body quickly enough to allow cooling to take place. An early indication that someone is starting to suffer from hyperthermia is heat exhaustion. The symptoms include a fast, weak pulse and rapid breathing, accompanied by heavy sweating.

If it worsens and becomes heat stroke, the skin will typically become hot and dry. Other signs and symptoms can vary with individuals but include dehydration, vomiting (causing greater dehydration), headaches and dizziness. In severe cases, the behaviour of the casualty makes them appear intoxicated, confused or hostile. Seizures are not uncommon as their condition deteriorates.

The initial treatment is to remove the underlying cause. For mild hyperthermia, cooling down by sitting in a shaded place, along with increased water intake is usually enough. If the condition is worse than mild, a good method of cooling the casualty is to remove excess clothing and dampen remaining clothes with cool water. Do not immerse the casualty in the sea as the shock could cause other complications. Generally, when someone has suffered from hyperthermia, professional medical assistance is required as soon as practical.

Measures can be taken to lessen the likelihood of succumbing to heatstroke. If the weather is very warm, don't dress for immersion in the water. If you do, you will heat up inside your drysuit and even cooling off in the water will not be enough. Make sure that you drink enough cool fluids – between 500ml and one litre per hour is recommended.

If you have to paddle to keep to a schedule, then try to do so in the morning or evening and keep out of the sun during the middle of the day when it is hottest. Seek shade often, to allow your body's thermostat time to recover to its normal state.

COLD INJURIES (HYPOTHERMIA)

Hypothermia is the main cold-related injury and there are two types which are of interest to us. The first is radiation hypothermia caused by the body losing heat to the surrounding air. This is insidious and typically happens over a long time period with the symptoms coming on gradually. If it is recognised early, it is possible to warm the casualty enough to stop the condition worsening.

The second type is immersion hypothermia caused, as the name suggests, by immersion in water. This is more serious, as the onset is much quicker and warming is more difficult. Immersion hypothermia takes around 20 to 40 minutes to develop in a normal adult. The *Cold Water Immersion* chapter gives much more information on hypothermia.

OTHER COMMON CONDITIONS AND INJURIES

The following are preventable, but sometimes they can come on quickly as with hypogly-caemia and friction blisters, even in people who do not normally suffer from these issues. The other two typically develop over a longer period of time with surfer's ear taking years to develop.

HYPOGLYCAEMIA

Hypoglycaemia is a condition when there isn't enough fuel in the body to enable it to function correctly. Most people who are prone to this generally know it, and have high energy snacks easily available. It often presents much like hypothermia and can be difficult to determine as the two often go hand in hand.

Selection of snacks.

FRICTION BLISTERS

These typically appear on the hands and are caused by gripping the paddle too tightly. Isolate the blister by wrapping with protective tape to prevent worsening. I like electrical insulation tape as it stretches and will stick to itself.

Electrical insulation tape on fingers to stop friction blisters.

SURFER'S EAR

This is a medical condition known as 'exostosis of the external auditory canal'. It develops through exposure to cold water and cold air over a long period of time. The ear canal becomes restricted by bony lumps, and water can get trapped behind these lumps, causing an infection to take hold. This condition does not stop you from paddling but you will need surgery. After the operation, you will need a few weeks without immersion in water. The treatment involves drilling the ear canal to make it the correct size again.

Prevention is best, and good quality earplugs will stop the formation of the bony lumps. A close-fitting neoprene hood worn while practising rolling and rescues will also reduce the problem.

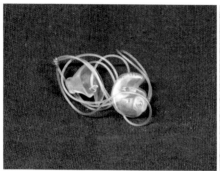

Earplugs and a neoprene hood to help prevent surfer's ear.

TENOSYNOVITIS OR PADDLER'S WRIST

The synovia or sheath that surrounds the wrist tendon becomes inflamed and prevention is the only cure. It is mostly caused by too tight a grip on the paddle shaft, but can also occur with excessive side-to-side movement of the wrist. Another cause is having a paddle shaft that is too large for your grip or wearing gloves, which has the same effect as the paddle shaft being too large. Tight wrist gaskets on your cag or drysuit can also be a cause.

At the onset, cold water can stop the initial symptoms from displaying. The first sign is often a 'creaking' sensation, especially over the top of the wrist where a watch would be worn. Strapping, supports and anti-inflammatory cream or tablets provide some relief, but the only true cure is to stop paddling until the body recovers.

Waiting, watching.
Photo: Michaela MacDonald

Boat damage (above) and subsequent repair (right).

Equipment

We were paddling as a group of twelve along the west coast of Lewis in the Outer Hebrides looking for rock hopping opportunities. There was a good swell running and as a group we were making decisions about where was safe and where was not. A good slot was found and I paddled through on the crest of the swell, steering left as I approached the rock at the centre of it.

From the rock, there was only really the option of going left, as the right channel would probably mean a foray high onto the rocks. I bumped my stern on the exit and turned around to see the next paddler already partway through and going right. I stayed in position in case a rescue was needed. Fortunately it was not, though the kayak was bounced about.

The next paddler had seen all this happening and started his approach carefully. Unfortunately this meant that he was too slow and his forward momentum was minimal when the wave crested and then drained, leaving the kayak sitting in a small pool of water.

The next wave lifted the kayak and slammed it against the rock. For several waves the kayak and paddler were kept in the same position, sometimes upright and sometimes inverted. There were lots of breaking fibreglass noises and when finally the paddler was flushed out towards me, the look of relief on his face was memorable.

Fortunately he was not injured but a quick check of the kayak revealed a crack on the hull behind the cockpit. As landing was not possible, we backtracked until we could go ashore safely. By this time the kayak was almost completely submerged.

Ashore, we gathered all of the repair materials we had as a group and set about fixing the damage. It took two full rolls of duct tape, two sheets of polythene, a group shelter, two air bags and more than a bit of patience to carry out the repair. When we launched again, we paddled another thirteen miles to our landing spot and the repairs held sufficiently well to keep water out.

As master, navigator, engineer, crewman (and engine), a kayaker must carry suitable equipment for his safety and needs, and this has to be accessible when necessary. Some items must be kept where they are reachable while sitting in the cockpit, and others can be stored in a hatch and accessed while rafted with another kayaker or ashore.

Of course what is carried is a personal choice that will depend on many factors, but as a general rule, to keep safe, each person should have a minimum of equipment that they **always** carry. There are many places and ways in which to carry this essential equipment.

Although the following reads like a checklist, this is not the intention. Certain items might be left out depending on the conditions. For example you don't need anything to deal with jellyfish stings in the UK if you are paddling in the winter, and a neoprene hood would be excessive in the tropics. Other items might be considered as 'group equipment', you might for example, find it quite adequate to carry two first aid kits between a group of five paddlers.

ON THE BODY

The most obvious place to keep items ready to hand is on your body. Wear a buoyancy aid (BA) or another type of personal flotation device (PFD). This must conform to the regulations of the country you are paddling in and be comfortable to wear all day. It should have enough room to carry all that you need while on the water but not be so bulky that your ability to move is restricted. It should be brightly coloured and have retro-reflective patches so that it can be seen at night. Whatever you pack into your PFD is ultimately carried on your shoulders and this weight will possibly cause some discomfort. Additionally this cargo will somewhat lessen the buoyancy of your PFD.

The following is a list from which I choose what to carry on my body. Other people may choose to carry some of these items elsewhere as they find that the bulkiness / weight impairs their ability to paddle. It would be ironic if an accident happened because a paddler was unable to paddle effectively as they were carrying too much safety equipment in their buoyancy aid!

WHISTLE

A whistle is great for initially getting attention, and works well for signalling between members of a group. It works best when the person who is to hear the signal is close by. Unfortunately, its use is limited in wind or close to breaking water, as the sound can become muffled.

COMPASS

Any orienteering-type compass is suitable to have in a pocket, ready to take a bearing. Ideally the base plate should be long enough to measure a reasonable distance on a map or chart. It is worth remembering that the compass safe distance from any electronic device is one metre, so keep your compass away from items that contain electronics and especially anything with a loudspeaker, as the magnetic field can play havoc with direction finding.

WHITE LIGHT

For small craft, including kayaks, the ability to show an all-round white light at night is a legal obligation. A headtorch is probably the best way to achieve this and there are many available on the market which are waterproof enough to be useful. In poor visibility or darkness, this light must be available so that it can be turned on fast enough to prevent a collision.

DAY / NIGHT FLARE

It is always a good idea to carry a day / night flare on your body in case you get separated from your boat. This type of flare is only really useful for showing your position when another boat is in sight as neither end of the flare lasts very long when activated.

LASER FLARE

Laser flares are available in red or green, depending on which model you choose. A laser flare is visible from a long way off and works best in clear conditions. Its main usefulness is to guide rescuers, such as a lifeboat or helicopter, to you. It is also useful to locate other parties and equipment if equipped with retro-reflective patches as the beam is intense and the reflection substantial.

Laser flare.

KNIFE

A knife secured on the outside of the buoyancy aid, which is always accessible and ready to use, would be ideal but in practice, it always seems to get in the way and caught on things. Another option is to have a line cutter attached externally and a locking / folding knife easily accessible in a pocket.

Folding knife.

Line cutter.

TAPE

Electrical tape is waterproof and will stick to itself. It is good for stopping blisters resulting from friction and for minor first aid and, as it is slightly elastic, it will give more than duct tape will.

BASIC FIRST AID KIT (OUCH-POUCH)

- ◎ A couple of stainless steel nappy pins for securing things easily.

- ◎ Elastoplast to provide padding before applying electrical tape.

- ◎ Steristrips for field stitching a bigger cut.

- ◎ A large field dressing if someone has a cut that needs to be dealt with while afloat. These dressings are big and absorbent and come in a sealed sterile package. Once opened, they need to be kept as dry as possible as a wet dressing will not stop blood flow as effectively.

- ◎ Medical gloves to protect yourself from the casualty, these are also useful to make a waterproof glove to protect a hand wound.

BASIC REPAIR KIT

◎ Flashband or Denso tape patches in a ziplock bag.

◎ A cloth and medical gloves in a separate ziplock bag. Use the cloth to dry the kayak and the gloves to keep your fingers clean.

VHF RADIO

A VHF (Very High Frequency) handheld radio is a means of two-way communication, either within a group or with external agencies. Some models are waterproof whereas others will need to be kept in a dry bag.

To legally use a VHF radio in the UK, you should be licensed. The great advantage of a radio over flares and locator beacons is that when asking for help you can be precise about your situation. Rescuers can also let you know what they are doing. Licensing and use of the VHF radio is covered in the *Rescue by Outside Agencies* chapter.

STROBE

When carried high on a shoulder a strobe is a very useful means of being located, especially at night and from above. A bicycle LED lamp also works well as the 'on' part of the flash is of a longer duration than the strobe. A marine strobe will be more waterproof than a bicycle lamp.

It's much better to have a dedicated strobe rather than one that also incorporates a torch or flashlight. If you have decided on a combined torch and strobe, be very aware that every time you use the light function, you will be lessening the time the rescue strobe will operate for.

Strobe.

KARABINER

A karabiner can be used for quick attachment in many situations and can help during towing set-ups. Know where it is so that you can clip yourself to anything available – deck lines, towlines, other karabiners or anything else you can think of, if the need arises. Knowing where it is may also stop you getting accidentally clipped to any of these things.

LENGTH OF CORD

A two-metre length of 3mm to 4mm cord can be used in many situations where you have to improvise. For example, I've used it to attach a deck line to a front toggle as the furthest-forward recessed deck fitting had pulled out, leaving a loop of rope trailing in the water. It is also useful as an extra deck line if required, and to secure a hatch cover.

LAMINATED ICE (IN CASE OF EMERGENCY) CARD

Make up an identification card with your details and laminate it. Important details to include on your ICE card: name, home address, date of birth, blood group, any known allergies (if none write 'no known allergies'), any regular medications, emergency contact name and number. Ensure it is kept up-to-date and is able to be read.

The card will also double as a jellyfish sting remover. Jellyfish stings stay attached to the skin with barbs and the poison sac fires every time they are touched. To remove them, 'shave' the area which has been stung by sliding the edge of the laminated card across the skin.

The card can also be used as a reinforcing patch to cover a small hole in a kayak before applying some tape to secure it.

SACHET(S) OF VINEGAR

Vinegar is another useful treatment for jellyfish stings. After using the laminated card to shave the area, apply vinegar. The acid in the vinegar neutralises the alkali of the jellyfish venom.

DOG-LEAD

Used for towing but can have other uses too.

STIRRUP

For assisting a casualty out of the water.

SURF WAX

Surf wax rubbed onto the paddle shaft gives a greater grip especially if your hands are slippery after applying sunscreen.

It also works well as a temporary repair putty on all types of kayak and as a plug for a holed spraydeck when 'riveted' through the material.

PLB – PERSONAL LOCATOR BEACON

A PLB is ideal for drawing the attention of the rescue services to your need for urgent help. PLBs are required to be registered and this registration kept up-to-date. In the UK and at the time of writing, this is with the UK Beacon Registry who keep a log of the information you provide. When the beacon is activated, anywhere in the world, Falmouth Coastguard trigger a rescue mission. As the signal is transmitted via satellite, there are fewer reception issues than with a VHF radio. The communication is one-way though, and there is no way of knowing if help is coming.

Personal locator beacon (PLB).

SNACKS

High calorie snacks are handy for when energy levels are getting depleted. If carrying anything with nuts in, take care in case another person has an allergy which could be triggered through contact. Energy gels are a good minimum bulk option, they are easy to take and give a boost.

CLOSE TO HAND

In the day hatch, knee hatch, deck bag or attached to the deck. Bear in mind that heavy deck bags raise your centre of gravity and increase the risk of a capsize.

- ◎ More food
- ◎ Thermos with hot drink
- ◎ First aid kit
- ◎ Repair kit
- ◎ Emergency hatch covers
- ◎ Storm cag
- ◎ Group shelter
- ◎ Plastic bivvy bag
- ◎ Warm jacket
- ◎ Warm hat

- ◎ Neoprene gloves and hand warmers
- ◎ Neoprene hood
- ◎ Insulated sit mat

ON THE DECK – BUT STILL REACHABLE WHILE SITTING

- ◎ Spare (split) paddles (ideally these should be the same as your main paddle, as if you have to use them, you will want the best you can afford).
- ◎ Flares (a minimum of one each: smoke, pinpoint and parachute).
- ◎ Navigation equipment: chart / map, long rule, chinagraph / grease pencil, length of string for measuring distance.
- ◎ A deck-mounted compass is a good idea if you are planning any long-distance paddling and especially if a crossing is being considered. Many of today's current kayaks have a recess to take a compass forward of the front deck hatch. In my opinion, this is just too far forward to be of much use. Around the toes is a much better place but not always easy to achieve. Any figures on the compass should be easy to read during the day and also at night.
- ◎ Contact tow
- ◎ Deck tow (if fitted)
- ◎ Paddle float (unless carried behind seat)
- ◎ Pump
- ◎ Sea anchor or drogue

REPAIR KIT

A repair kit is of little use in itself, unless you know how to use it. The same goes to say with the rest of your equipment; learn how to use it and be inventive when needed.

We don't always have the opportunity to practise breakages for real, and have to make do with simulations instead. Learn to repair your kit in a controlled environment to start with, this will help you become adaptable and able to repair most damaged or broken items. You don't want to be repairing your first skeg control at night in the wind and rain.

REPAIR KIT CONTENTS

Roll of duct tape – Carry a full roll in your repair kit. It is unlikely that a short length wrapped around a pencil will be enough to carry out a repair of any sort.

Flashband patches – These stick well to a dry kayak but not so well if there is a lot of moisture about. Available from hardware stores.

Denso tape patches on plastic fabric backing – Denso tape is available from hardware stores. Prepare a few patches at home, and for ease of handling, store them on a piece of plastic. Denso tape patches will stick to everything whether it is wet or dry. Have a pair of protective gloves available for handling the tape because it is messy, and a stiff piece of plastic for pressing the gooey fabric onto the repair.

Cloth for drying the kayak – A simple J cloth works well.

Multi-tool and / or other suitable tools – Make sure you have a tool for each fitting on the kayak.

Spare skeg or rudder control wire – Plus the knowledge of how to replace it if damaged.

Copper wire – This can be used for binding or stitching a broken kayak or paddle.

Dental floss or sailmaker's twine – For sewing repairs.

Strong needle – Kept in a cork protector.

Length of strong cord – Has many uses.

Plastic sheet – To reinforce a kayak repair where tape on its own would not be sufficiently strong. I use a piece cut from a 5 litre container.

Abrasive paper – To roughen an area before a repair, or to smooth any rough edges of a broken kayak or damaged paddle, or even a sharp cockpit rim.

Instant epoxy glue – This type of glue sets in five minutes and is waterproof.

Cling film or pallet wrap – This can be wrapped around a kayak as a temporary repair for a badly-leaking skeg box, split kayak or even a lost hatch cover.

FIRST AID KIT

First aid and the contents of a first aid kit are important, as the sea kayaker is often a long way from medical care. It is worth taking an advanced first aid training course such as a 'wilderness emergency medical technician' or a 'wilderness first responder' type of course. These give more in-depth knowledge to the first aider than a conventional first aid course and assume that professional medical help is not close to hand.

As a minimum, a first aid kit should comprise enough equipment to stop something bleeding excessively, hold things together that are cut or broken, and keep the user safe. It should also contain non-prescription drugs that will control pain to a limited degree.

A first aid kit must be dry and easy to use. To ensure dryness I use two dry bags with a pair of protective gloves inside the first bag. This means that if dealing with a bleeding wound, I can put on the gloves even before I get inside the bag with the first aid kit.

FIRST AID KIT CONTENTS

- 2 pairs examination gloves
- 2 large trauma dressings
- 2 small trauma dressings
- 1 roll of micropore
- Absorbent dressings
- Non-adhesive dressings
- Sticking plasters
- 2 triangular bandages
- 2 small bandages
- 2 large elastic bandages
- Large safety pins
- A small white light
- 300mg dispersible aspirin
- 400mg ibuprofen (personal use)
- 500mg paracetamol (personal use)

Important note – as a first aider you are not allowed to 'prescribe' drugs of any type because of the possibility of someone having a bad reaction to the medication. The exception is aspirin; which can be given to people having a suspected heart attack. Get them to chew and swallow one normal adult aspirin (300mg) which will increase their chances of survival. Aspirin is a form of anticoagulant, so allows the blood to flow more easily. There are side effects associated with aspirin, but these are outweighed by the positive benefits when administered to someone having a heart attack.

PUMPS

A suitable pump should be carried when on the water and there are several options available. It must be useable while sitting in the kayak, and ideally also to help empty other kayaks. It has to be robust enough to endure repeated immersion in the sea as well as cope with sand being flushed through it.

TYPES OF PUMP

Stirrup – These are the cheapest, most portable and probably most reliable pumps available to sea kayakers. It can easily be passed to others who are paddling alongside, a plus point. There are several types available, with the most sturdy ones equipped with a stainless steel shaft. This adds a bit of weight but makes them substantially stronger than the slightly cheaper all-plastic versions. If it doesn't already come equipped with a flotation collar, make one, and make sure it is tied on to save it being lost to Neptune. All stirrup pumps sink when full of water.

When using the pump, short strokes are preferable to longer ones as they place less stress on the shoulder and the pump itself. Often the kayak being emptied will have to be tilted to allow the remaining water to flow to one side and the pump placed in the deepest area. The outlet has to be turned away from the rescuer and casualty otherwise they will both get a shower of cold, salty water.

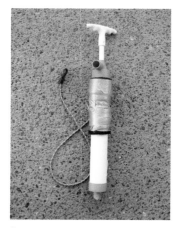

It is possible to replace the spraydeck to stop more water getting into the cockpit and insert the pump either through the side or the waist entry. It is easy to add more pumps to the situation to remove the water more quickly.

Stirrup pump.

Electric pumps – These come in two main types, both with the drawback that they have batteries which need to be charged, not to mention the risks of corrosion of the often delicate electrical contacts.

The first is a portable type designed for the bilges of sailing boats. It comes with a weight attached so that it will sink to the bottom of the inside of the hull. Unfortunately, it will also sink to the bottom of the ocean unless the ballast plate is removed and a piece of cord attached to secure the pump to the kayak. Like the stirrup pump, this type can be moved from kayak to kayak and is therefore useful in a group.

Electric fitted pump. Photo: Rowland Woollven

The second is a permanent fixture within the kayak. It requires a power source, a switch, an inlet at the lowest point in the cockpit, an outlet, and the means to easily charge it. It is complicated, but in the situation where you need a hands-free pumping solution, this has to be one of the best options. The pump is generally fitted behind the seat with the inlet fixed into a shaped foam block at the lowest point in the kayak. The outlet is on the deck orientated so that no one will get a shower. A sealed battery box is attached to the inside of the day hatch with velcro, and the wires pass through the bulkhead and are sealed to stop water moving from the cockpit to the day hatch. A switch is normally fitted on the deck and, depending on the type, may have a protective cover over the top to prevent accidental operation or damage to the switch.

Foot-operated pump – This adds weight forward in the kayak and can make handling difficult. The pump is mounted on the front bulkhead with the pickup tube running along the centre of the hull. Again the outlet is on the deck. The bulkhead needs to be built much stronger to cope with the added pressure placed on it when using the pump so this adds weight too. It is possible to empty the kayak while paddling or at least supporting yourself.

Hand-operated pumps – Few kayaks now come with hand pumps, either front or rear deck mounted. Both options require a hand to operate, rendering the paddler unable to paddle or support themselves.

SEA ANCHOR (DROGUE)

A sea anchor or drogue is a piece of fabric towed behind the kayak to slow down the drift or stabilise direction. It is probably most useful for a leader when in charge of larger groups.

It can be used to slow the drift of a raft or a rescue, and is almost invaluable when towing a raft in a strong following wind and needing to reach an area of safety rather than pass it.

STEERING A RAFT

Without a sea anchor, it is possible to steer a raft (particularly if it is a small one) from behind by positioning the bow of your kayak between two of the kayaks in the raft, but directional control is limited. Limited directional control, downwind, can also be achieved if the two people on the outside of the raft perform a stern rudder while being held by those in the middle of the raft.

There are two main types of sea anchor for kayaks; the cone type and the 'handkerchief' or square type. The cone has a larger opening at the leading end and the smaller exit normally has a draw cord to reduce the size of the opening. Deploying from a kayak is quite straightforward. These cone sea anchors are normally quite large and not as efficient as the smaller, square handkerchief type.

The handkerchief sea anchor that I have found to be most satisfactory is approximately 30cm by 30cm with reinforcing tape stitched diagonally across the corners and with a small hole in the centre that stabilises the whole thing while in use. The tape extends and forms the attachment point for the line. I have a five-metre line ending in a screw shackle as I have found that simple clips always manage to free themselves.

If you want to place the drogue further away from the kayaks being towed, you can add a waist or boat tow into the system. This can be easily adjusted but there is risk of losing the tow system.

Adding a small float at the CROSS-OVER tapes where the small hole is, allows the drogue to surface when the pressure is released.

'Handkerchief' type drogue.

APPENDIX A: COMMON AND LESS COMMON INCIDENTS

Below is a list of incidents I have either had to deal with, or know of someone else who has. Some of them are fairly common and happen often, others are much less common and you would be unlucky if you were involved in them. These are in addition to the fairly simple 'group member capsizes' type of incident and does not include those incidents brought about by weather or tidal abnormalities. I've starred the ones that I feel are more common and that you will be more likely to have to deal with.

EQUIPMENT RELATED

Hatch cover being flipped off *

Lost hatch cover *

Damaged hatch cover *

Hatch rim detached from kayak

Jammed skeg (up or down) *

Broken skeg

Broken skeg control *

Damaged skeg wire *

Skeg falling out of kayak

Skeg punched up through skeg box

Broken deck line *

Broken deck elastic *

Broken toggle cord *

Gel coat chipped *

Deck fitting pulled out

Deck separated from hull

Cockpit rim detached

End of plastic kayak cut off

Plastic kayak folded and cracked

End of composite kayak smashed

Composite kayak broken around rock

Composite kayak broken in dumping surf

Hole on hull of kayak from rock *

Kayak punctured by other kayak

Bulkhead detached

Foam bulkhead pivoting

Footrest coming off track *

Complete footrest failure

Backrest failure *

Seat support breaking

Seat-securing screws coming loose

Rudder control wire breaking

Rudder stuck in up or down position

Loose line in cockpit *

Broken paddle blade

Broken paddle shaft

Broken paddle centre joint

Lost paddle

Boat floating off

Holed spraydeck, cag, trousers, drysuit *

Spraydeck imploding

Lost spraydeck

Pan with holes in

Stove not working

Flat batteries in: strobe, torch, VHF radio *

Pump handle broken off

Electric pump flat battery

Dropped glasses, car keys, headtorch, VHF

Towing cleat pulled out

Towing cleat seized

Quick-release buckle on towline broken

Deck-mounted compass smashed

Battery terminals corroded

Broken tent poles

Damaged tent fabric, punctured or burned

Punctured thermarest

Lost map or chart *

INJURY OR ILLNESS RELATED

Dislocated shoulder

Dislocated knee

Crushed hand

Migraine headache

Epilepsy episode

Unconscious still in kayak

Hand cut with sharp knife *

Cuts from barnacles, mussels or rock *

Tenosynovitis or paddler's wrist *

Hypothermia *

Hyperthermia *

Hypoglycaemia *

Hypohydration *

Heart attack or suspected heart attack

Asthma attack

Twisted ankle or knee *

Broken ribs due to collision in surf

Cut on forehead below helmet due to collision in tide race

Broken nose due to water bottle being washed off deck in surf

Lacerated thumb due to being caught in towline D ring

Stroke

Seasickness *

Anxiety attack *

Blisters on hands *

Salt sores and chafing *

Friction burns from rope *

Finger nail torn off

Fish hook in hand

Detached biceps tendon

Exhaustion

Fibreglass splinters *

Jellyfish stings *

Finger trapped in toggle loop

Burns and scalds *

Tick attached to skin *

Lost contact lenses

Badly bruised eye due to nose clips on elastic hitting casualty in eye

TOWLINE RELATED

Towline wrapped around legs

Towline clip seized *

Towline does not float

Towline not restrained on rear deck, loose rope.

Towline made from 50 metres of 2mm spectra cord

Towline made from 5 metres of 12mm polypropylene crab pot line

Towline caught on:

    Flares *

    Pump *

    End of kayak *

    Spare paddles *

    Bridge pillar

    Buoy

I suggest, from the list, work out how you might go about dealing with a chosen incident and then test it with a group of friends making sure to review what went well and what needs to be changed.

APPENDIX B: SELECTED BIBLIOGRAPHY

BOOKS

Kayak Rolling, (2004) Collins, L. Pesda Press, Wales. ISBN 0953195686

Oxford Handbook of Expedition and Wilderness Medicine, (2015) Oxford University Press 2nd edition, England. ISBN 9780199688418

Researching Your Own Practice – The Discipline of Noticing, (2002) Mason, J. Routledge-Falmer, England. ISBN 0415248620

Sea Kayak, (2006) Brown, G. Pesda Press, Wales. ISBN 095470617X

Sea Kayak Navigation, (2007) Ferrero, F. Pesda Press 2nd edition, Wales. ISBN 9781906095031

Sources of Power, How People Make Decisions, (1999) Klein, G. The MIT Press, USA. ISBN 9780262611466

The Checklist Manifesto: How to get things right, (2011) Gawande, A. Profile Books, USA. ISBN 9781846683145

DVDS

Sea Kayak with Gordon Brown – DVD series, (2013) Sunart Media, Scotland. www.seakayakwithgordonbrown.com

ACADEMIC PAPERS

O'Connor, P. and Flin, R. (2003) *'Crew resource management training for offshore oil production teams.'* Safety Science 41, 111–129

McCammon, I. (2002) *Evidence of heuristic traps in recreational avalanche incidents.* Presented at the International Snow Science Workshop, Penticton, British Columbia, Sept. 30–Oct 4, 2002